D0016748

Today & Forever

TODAY AND FOREVER

Copyright © 1989, Leroy Brownlow
Brownlow Publishing Company,
6309 Airport Freeway,
Fort Worth, TX 76117

All rights reserved. The use or reprinting
of any part of this book without the express written
permission of the publisher is prohibited.

Printed in the United States of America.

Gift Edition: ISBN 0-915720-93-0
Trade Edition: ISBN 0-915720-94-9
Leather Edition: ISBN 0-915720-95-7

10 9 8 7 6 5 4 3

THIS BOOK
BELONGS TO

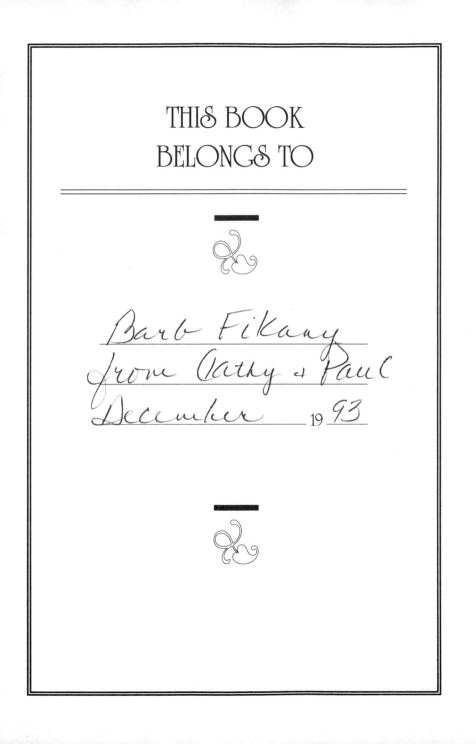

Barb Fikany
from Cathy & Paul
December 19 93

Today & Forever

*Daily Strength
for a Brighter
Tomorrow*

Leroy Brownlow

BROWNLOW PUBLISHING CO., INC.

Other Brownlow Gift Books

A Few Hallelujahs for Your Ho-Hums
A Psalm in My Heart
As a Man Thinketh
Better Than Medicine—A Merry Heart
Children Won't Wait
Flowers for Mother
Flowers for You
Flowers of Friendship
Flowers That Never Fade
For Mom With Love
Give Us This Day
Grandpa Was a Preacher
It's a One-derful Life
Just Between Friends
Leaves of Gold
Love Is Forever
Making the Most of Life
The Fruit of the Spirit
The Greatest Thing in the World
The Other Wise Man
Thoughts of Gold—Wisdom for Living
Today & Forever
Today Is Mine
University of Hard Knocks

Foreword

In a quest for the best for man, the author presents 366 original essays, designed for a year of daily meditations or devotions, and supports each with a relevant quotation from some great and renowned mind that has made his or her way into recorded history, plus a pertinent Scripture. This unique format of triple declarations on the same topic adds strength and credence to what is said. It allows three sources to come to a focal point on the same subject.

This is the author's twenty-eighth book, four of which are daily messages of direction, help and inspiration: *Today Is Mine*, *A Psalm in My Heart*, *Give Us This Day*, and this one, *Today and Forever*.

In this volume the reader will find light—let it shine; a ladder—climb it; nourishment—let the cup run over; enrichment more precious than gold— let the treasures be yours; and hope— cling to it.

A studied effort has been made in this book to give clarification, insight, depth, ideals, inspiration and motivation— presented in simple language—to help us all arrive at safe destinations and higher peaks in our pilgrimages to a brighter tomorrow. If these ambitions have been achieved, then these pages will have the power to elevate us all. For what lifts me lifts thee.

LEROY BROWNLOW

Let Us Resolve

We don't do better accidentally. This means that we must purpose and plan to go on to better things. The fact that we occasionally break a resolution should not stop us. When we break the water pitcher we don't quit drinking water. Therefore, let us resolve what we ought and perform what we resolve.

I will start afresh each new day with a higher,
*   fairer creed;*
I will cease to stand complaining of my ruthless
*   neighbor's greed;*
I will cease to sit repining while my duty's call
*   is clear;*
I will waste no moment whining, and my heart
*   shall know no fear.*

I will not be swayed by envy when my rival's
*   strength is shown;*
I will not deny his merit, but I'll try to prove
*   my own;*
I will try to see the beauty spread before me,
*   rain or shine;*
I will cease to preach your duty and be more
*   concerned with mine.*

—AUTHOR UNKNOWN

And Solomon determined to build a house for the name of the Lord.

—II CHRONICLES 2:1

Moved by Zeal

I t is fitting in the early part of the year that we reflect on zeal. For it is a most necessary quality. It sparks life and puts it in motion. Zeal, however, needs knowledge, or it will pull the trigger when the gun is only half cocked. Also, if it lacks tolerance, it can fuel extreme fanaticism. It is a good horse to carry us, but it definitely needs a bridle. Without it, we are on a runaway horse.

"We spend our years as a tale that is told." One day the last words will have to be written, "The end." And zeal will greatly affect what goes into the story.

Zeal is like fire; it needs both feeding and watching.

—AUTHOR UNKNOWN

But it is good to be zealously affected always in a good thing....

—GALATIANS 4:18

Safe Harbors

I t's a mark of wisdom to pursue a safe course. That's why we put fire escapes in buildings, traffic signals on streets, and speed limits on highways; why we have physicals, take blood pressure, inspect meat, build houses on the rock, read what we sign and especially the small print, and search the Scriptures to learn if the things we hear are so.

Sometimes blind and impulsive rashness pays, but think how often it fails. If self-preservation is the first law of life, then safety would have to be the second. And the first question to ask concerning any investment is not how much it will make but how safe is it.

Let us run into a safe harbor.

—ALCAEUS
(625-575 B.C.)

The wise in heart shall be called prudent.
—PROVERBS 16:21

Seeds of Today

Today provides the memories of yesterday and sets the stage for tomorrow. A big day! Filled with opportunity! Loaded with responsibility! However, it is not today that drives us mad; it is the hangovers from yesterday and the worries of tomorrow.

So the big word in living is *today.* And logically, it should be our most successful day, for we have all the yesterdays as instructors. Let us fill today with happiness, beauty, service, helpfulness, unselfishness, forgiveness, courage, neighborliness, love, and devotion to a great cause. Treat it as a sacred trust. Treat it conscientiously, for it is quickly dying into a yesterday, which can give pleasant memories to enliven us or fearful ghosts to haunt us. Live today! Tomorrow—tomorrow may be too late to live.

All the flowers of all the tomorrows are in the seeds of today.

—ANONYMOUS

And, behold, as thy life was much set by this day.

—I SAMUEL 26:24

Flowers of Forgiveness

Forgiveness is the scent that flowers give when they are trampled. It's something we all need, "for all have sinned and come short of the glory of God." Moreover, it's a goodness we need to extend to others, for if you "forgive not men their trespasses, neither will your Father forgive your trespasses."

Forgiveness blots out the infraction. When God forgives sin, He remembers it no more forever. Forgiveness doesn't bring it up again; if it does, it's not forgiveness. It puts things back like they were before the breach occurred. When it buries the hatchet, it doesn't leave the handle sticking out.

Doing an injury puts you below your enemy;
Revenging one makes you but even with him;
Forgiving it sets you above him.
—BENJAMIN FRANKLIN

...forgive us our debts, as we forgive our debtors.
—MATTHEW 6:12

Safe Upon the Rock

L ife gets shaky when our foundation is weak. In the long run, no person, cause, or institution can stand longer than his or its foundation. The strength of either is proportionate to its base; and the higher the superstructure, the stronger it must be.

If it's foolish to build a house on sand, it's even more foolish to build a life on trash. If a person's foundation does not include the elements of ambition, industry, goodwill, trustworthiness, loyalty, ethics, righteousness, faith, hope, love and reverence for God and respect for man, he is sure to see his life collapse and fall under the weight of weakness.

Safe upon the solid rock the ugly houses stand:
Come and see the shining palace built upon the
sand.

—EDNA ST. VINCENT MILLAY

Laying up in store for themselves a good foundation against the time to come, that they may lay hold on eternal life.

—I TIMOTHY 6:19

When Extremism Is Not Extreme

T o be considered an extremist can be either a compliment or a censure, depending upon one's general tenor of life and the issue involved. Some matters are of such nature that they must be held inviolately, though one may be slurred as an extremist, while other issues of lesser importance can be compromised without violating conscience.

The Apostle Paul was accused of being mad, an insane radical. But there is a difference between a person with uncompromising convictions and a fanatic with self-centered stubbornness. We are commanded, "Stand fast in the faith," and to some people, this makes us extremists. Thanks for the compliment!

Moderation in temper is always a virtue; but moderation in principle is always a vice.

—THOMAS PAINE

...O man greatly beloved, fear not: peace be unto thee; be strong, yea, be strong.

—DANIEL 10:19

Yellow Lights

"Look before you leap." In jumping, be sure you won't mind the landing; in walking, that the pathway is not thorny; in picking friends, that they won't lower you; in signing a paper, that you're not bankrupting yourself; and in driving, that you're not going to your own funeral.

Where there is little caution, there is much trouble. Forethought is foreprotected. Be not overly cautious, however, or you will never do anything wrong or right. Study the matter, chew on it, sleep on it, and then decide. Certainly some mistakes will be made, but he who makes no mistakes makes nothing.

Caution is the eldest child of wisdom.

—VICTOR HUGO

But watch thou in all things.

—II TIMOTHY 4:5

A Faithful Friend

There is no finer tonic than a faithful friend. He lifts your spirit and rejuvenates your life. He is true, but a false friend is as dangerous as an avowed enemy. A true friend speaks well of you behind your back. He bears your infirmities and is there when the need arises. No fair-weather companion! He is your nearest and surest relation, though you and he may not be blood kin. Hold to your friends; even if you have a thousand, you have none to spare. Never wound, abuse or exploit a friend. Remember, the only way to have and keep a friend is to be one.

A real friend is one who walks in when the rest of the world walks out.

—WALTER WINCHELL

A friend loveth at all times, and a brother is born for adversity.

—PROVERBS 17:17

School of Experience

 He knows the water best who has swum in it. Experience is worth more than mere theory and bare book learning. Truths digested in textbooks are not fully learned until they are brought home to us in actual living. Experience takes us beyond the limits of a book.

So, in the last analysis, the most learned are the most experienced. They know the ins and the outs, the ups and the downs. And where some are going, they have already been. It's the School of Experience. The tuition is very high, and payment must be made in full. But there is no other way to get it for any less.

Only so much do I know, as I have lived.
—RALPH WALDO EMERSON

...I have learned by experience that the Lord hath blessed me for thy sake.
—GENESIS 30:27

More Blessed to Give

Since "it is more blessed to give than to receive," then we ought not to let others get all the better blessings. This puts us on the giving end instead of the receiving end. The most precious gift is self. When self is given, the giving of materials becomes a matter of the heart, an act of love, not a slavish or ritualistic act prompted solely by a sense of duty.

Giving wisely, however, is no easy task. If it enslaves the recipient, it does more harm than good. So while we give to the needy, let's also raise them up to where they won't need it. For independence is a cherished state.

Whatever I have given I still possess.
— LATIN PROVERB

...for God loveth a cheerful giver.
— II CORINTHIANS 9:7

Reach for a Star

 He who aims at nothing is sure to hit it. Goals, therefore, are essential to achievement. They are not mere dreams. They are objectives which provide commitment, spark, power and drive. No one finds meaning in life by just drifting. It's a look to the distant harbor and the set of the sails that give meaning and progress to the journey of life.

And as you act upon your goals, they act upon you. Ordinary goals keep people ordinary, so set your goals high enough. They become attainable—if reasonable—because as you reach for a star, your arm grows longer.

If you have built castles in the air, your work need not be lost, that is where they should be; now put the foundation under them.
                              —HENRY DAVID THOREAU

...this one thing I do, forgetting those things which are behind, and reaching forth unto those things which are before, I press toward the mark....
                              —PHILIPPIANS 3:13,14

Ease Is a Boresome State

There is too much talk about a life of ease. Smooth sailing does not make robust sailors. It is all right to improve means and methods, but to eliminate all effort and struggle is not beneficial. Many people have their troubles and worries because they expect life to be too easy. Take struggle out and out goes challenge and in comes boredom.

The unhappiest people in all the world are those on easy street. Most of us don't need lighter weights, just stronger backs. So let us pray and exercise to obtain strength equal to our tasks.

A life of ease is a difficult pursuit.
—WILLIAM COWPER

Woe to them that are at ease in Zion....
—AMOS 6:1

God, the First Cause

It is sensible to believe in God, hence the Apostle Paul appealed to common sense to prove the existence of God. In logical reasoning, he stated, "For every house is builded by some man; but he that built all things is God" (Hebrews 3:4). That makes sense! For no house could build itself, and no world could build itself.

The very heavens testify to the creative power of God. In recognition of God as the First Cause, David said, "The heavens declare the glory of God; and the firmament showeth his handiwork" (Psalm 19:1). A French infidel blatantly boasted, "We will pull down your churches; we will destroy everything that reminds you of God." Then a poor peasant replied, "But you will leave us the sun, the moon and the stars, and as long as they shine we shall have a reminder of God."

We are because God is.

—EMANUEL SWEDENBORG

In the beginning God created the heaven and the earth.

—GENESIS 1:1

A Wise Investment

I t pays to be good. This was the observation of Thoreau, who said, "Goodness is the only investment that never fails."

Goodness is like leaven hidden in three measures of meal. It's a permeating and modifying influence in our society. The good person makes others good, so one way to make the world better is to be good. Ten righteous souls would have saved Sodom. And another encouraging thing about goodness is it's within the reach of all. Of course we have to work at it; however, it comes easier than some people think because the more it is communicated, the more it grows.

Not all can be clever, but all can be good. If you can't be both, it's better to be good than brilliant.

Be good, sweet maid, and let who will be clever.
—CHARLES KINGSLEY

And I myself also am persuaded of you, my brethren, that ye also are full of goodness....
—ROMANS 15:14

Test of Ethics

E thics—a set of moral principles that govern a person in dealing with others. When followed, they give a person a dove attitude instead of a hawk attitude, a deportment of goodness instead of exploitation. A dog-eat-dog diet is sickening. There is no place for cannibalism, though it may be called opportunism, in an advanced society. Here is a test of business ethics: (1) Is it the whole truth? (2) Is it honest? (3) Is it fair to both parties? (4) Does it treat the other party the way you want to be treated? (5) Will it make you feel good when it's over? Pass these and your grade is A+.

I would rather be the man who bought the Brooklyn Bridge than the man who sold it.
—WILL ROGERS

And they said, Thou hast not defrauded us, nor oppressed us, neither hast thou taken aught of any man's hand.
—I SAMUEL 12:4

The Pillow of Conscience

A condemning conscience interferes with the enjoyment of wrong, but wrong is something no one should enjoy in the first place. Indeed, conscience is not an enemy but a friend, a protector of a better life. Thus the testimony of a good conscience is the softest pillow upon which any person has ever slept.

Even though we suffer censures from the world, a clear conscience will give us the assurance and strength to bear any trouble. It protects from fear and adds to bravery, while an evil "conscience does make cowards of us all."

The foundation of true joy is in the conscience.
—SENECA
(8 B.C.-A.D. 65)

And herein do I exercise myself, to have always a conscience void of offense toward God, and toward men.
—ACTS 24:16

Pure Religion

If there is a God—and there is—then it is sensible for us to be religious. Understandably, religion is evident the world over among all races, tribes and colors. For man, having a spirit, apparently seeks communion with the Great Spirit. Indeed, religion plays a great role in providing a stronger and happier life.

So religion is not something to endure but something that gives endurance. Not something to tolerate but something to tap. It is more than past tense; it is also present tense and future tense, something today and more tomorrow.

Religion should be the rule of life, not a casual incident of it.

—BENJAMIN DISRAELI

Pure religion and undefiled before God and the Father is this, To visit the fatherless and widows in their affliction, and to keep himself unspotted from the world.

—JAMES 1:27

Home and Family

Two of the deepest, richest words in our language are *home* and *family.* May we make them a domain of (1) Bible direction, (2) prayer, (3) authority, (4) love, (5) security, (6) togetherness, (7) helpfulness, (8) counsel, (9) tolerance, (10) responsibility, (11) concern, (12) unselfishness, (13) discipline, (14) peace, and (15) happiness.

When these attitudes prevail, home becomes a nest of love, a circle of strength, a fortress of protection, a body of togetherness, a channel of goodwill, a balm of healing, a refuge of renewal, a school of learning, and a star of hope.

Days come both good and bad, but a strong family is prepared for either: They can enjoy the good ones and handle the bad ones. It has no substitute.

The happiest moments of my life have been the few which I have passed at home in the bosom of my family.

—Thomas Jefferson

And, ye fathers, provoke not your children to wrath: but bring them up in the nurture and admonition of the Lord.

—Ephesians 6:4

Climbing Higher

Each of us has his mountain to climb, which tries his strength and determination. But there is no way to reach the top without climbing, for there are no elevators for life. It is either climb or remain at the lower level.

The best preparation for the ascent is to strengthen yourself for the task. See to it that you have an unyielding grip, steady feet, a strong heart, and an upward look. Also, be willing to take a slow pace, especially in slippery places. And finally, set your mind to enjoy the effort, for there can be as much fun in the climb as there is in standing on the summit.

No ascent is too steep for mortals.

—HORACE
(65-8 B.C.)

Who shall ascend into the hill of the Lord? Or who shall stand in his holy place? He that hath clean hands, and a pure heart; who hath not lifted up his soul unto vanity, nor sworn deceitfully.

—PSALM 24:3,4

Saved by Criticism

We put anti-knock in our gasoline tanks. I wish it were that easy to handle the knocks that come from human mouths. Do we justify the knocks we give others on the basis that they are constructive? It is easy to take the view that constructive criticism is when I criticize you, and destructive criticism is when you criticize me.

Nevertheless, there is more profit in being criticized than in criticizing. Still, there is a tendency to choose ruination by praise rather than salvation by criticism.

If a statue should ever be built to a critic, its hands would have to be filled with mud. No glory! Just a stark reminder!

Soiling another will never make one's self clean.
—ALFRED LORD TENNYSON

Thou therefore which teachest another, teachest thou not thyself?
—ROMANS 2:21

Waste and Want

To be worthy of what we receive, we must be preserving, unsquandering and thrifty. This can be done without being stingy and greedy. They are different topics.

Waste is seen in various ways: failure to take a stitch in time, neglect of clothes, improper care of food, castoff of materials still good and usable, needless burning of lights and gas, abuse of car, and time, perhaps the greatest waste of all.

There is neither grandeur nor luxury in wastefulness, just foolishness. The road of wastefulness leads to beggary. If waste controls us today, want is apt to possess us tomorrow.

And willful waste, depend upon't,
Brings, almost always, woeful want.

—JANE TAYLOR

And not many days after the younger son gathered all together...and wasted his substance.... And when he had spent all,...he began to be in want.

—LUKE 15:13,14

Keep Our Chin Up

O ne of the most tragic harmers in all the world is discouragement. Unless it is soon whipped, it can become the cause of many ills: It may invite defeat, stifle ambition, grow into envy, swell into resentment, and lead to dissipation. Being too downhearted to stand upright, we may fall for anything. Truly, despair may become the grave of dead hopes.

No matter what happens, keep our chins up and our eyes looking to the mountaintop. The bigger we are, the more it takes to discourage us. God lives. The world keeps turning. Don't get off, we can make it.

Life is the game that must be played:
This truth at least, good friends, we know;
So live and laugh, nor be dismayed
As one by one the phantoms go.
                              —EDWIN ARLINGTON ROBINSON

Wait on the Lord: be of good courage, and he shall strengthen thine heart....
                              —PSALM 27:14

Now Is the Time

The big word in life is *now*. It is the only time you can depend on. Life, the soul and the present moment are man's only possessions, and the latter should be used to enhance the former two. If the most sensible function of man is to live, then he cannot ignore the now. Tomorrow is only a fool's paradise. When you bring out the measure of life, bring out now. For it's not what you've done or what you're going to do but what you're doing now that counts.

Now's the day, and now's the hour.

—ROBERT BURNS

...behold, now is the accepted time; behold, now is the day of salvation.

—II CORINTHIANS 6:2

Unpretentious

What a compliment! Unfeigned. Not counterfeit. Not hypocritical. He is what he is. Means what he says. Not two-faced. Indeed, we are not actors on a make-believe stage; we are livers in a real world. No matter what might be feigned, reality brings each back to the real person he is.

Of course, hypocrisy has its present wages, but later the check will bounce. The biggest payoff in unfeignedness is the rewarding feeling that we are real, no fake. The best life is imperfect enough, so let's not feign; for by feigning we make it worse, but by sincerity we make it better.

I would be true, for there are those who trust me,
I would be pure, for there are those who care.
—HOWARD ARNOLD WALTER

Knowest thou not this of old, since man was placed upon earth, that the triumphing of the wicked is short, and the joy of the hypocrite but for a moment?
—JOB 20:4,5

Almost Is Not Good Enough

 lmost is good enough when it comes to hanging, but in most experiences it's a loser. Almost never won a battle, nor quit a bad habit, nor passed a course, nor got elected to office.

Obviously, almost is not good enough—unless we have done our best. In that case, though the reward for winning is not obtained, we still win for having tried our utmost. This makes us champions though we do not receive the blue ribbon. There are other ribbons.

"Almost" never killed a fly.

—GERMAN PROVERB

Then Agrippa said unto Paul, Almost thou persuadest me to be a Christian.

—ACTS 26:28

Sugared Poison

A flatterer is a person who would exploit us by appealing to our egotism. When he spreads the mush, just look at it. Don't swallow it. "For flattery," as Jonathan Swift said, "is the food of fools." Sugared poison, a poison that swells the head instead of the stomach. It is given by what looks like friends, but even wolves look like dogs. It is much safer to recognize facts, though uncomplimentary, than to gloat in hypocritical blarney. To believe the truth about ourselves is half the battle; the other half is to go from there in a commitment to improve.

Avoid flatterers, for they are thieves in disguise.
—WILLIAM PENN

A man that flattereth his neighbor spreadeth a net for his feet.
—PROVERBS 29:5

Ordained of God

I t is impossible to have a government without giving up some freedom; and thus the more we keep government at a minimum, the more freedom we have. The best government, therefore, is one that gives its people the broadest opportunity to work out their own destiny and to attain their own happiness.

Let's demand a government that treats all its citizens alike and one that is free of dishonesty, unfairness, favoritism, selfishness, dirty politics, and short-range thinking that considers only what's appealing at the moment. May we not sell our birthright to the highest bidder who buys our vote with our own tax money.

If citizens of a nation have too much greed on the one hand and too little dedication on the other to govern themselves, they face government by others. God forbid!

We have given you a Republic, if you can only keep it that.

—BENJAMIN FRANKLIN

Let every soul be subject unto the higher powers. For there is no power but of God: the powers that be are ordained of God.

—ROMANS 13:1

Tell Me No Lies

T he honorable person has nothing to fear from truth, but he certainly does from lies. Lies put words in his mouth he didn't utter, accuse him of doing things he didn't do, have him in places he didn't go, and attribute to him attitudes he didn't manifest.

Lies come in different colors and sizes: black lies, white lies, big lies, little lies, and half-truths. And a lie by any other name is still a lie. Regardless of shade or size or what it's called, it's still a misrepresentation of fact and a perversion of truth. It may be called a convenience in time of trouble, but time will prove it to be only a complication and a trust-breaker. Business, education, politics, religion—all things worthwhile—are crying out, *Tell me no lies.*

No man has a good enough memory to be a successful liar.

—ABRAHAM LINCOLN

Lying lips are abomination to the Lord: but they that deal truly are his delight.

—PROVERBS 12:22

The Measure of Greatness

One measurement of a tree is the fruit it produces, and this is the only true measurement of human greatness: good works that bless others. Such a person is "like a tree planted by the rivers of water, that bringeth forth his fruit in his season."

Definitely, true greatness is not dependent on degrees or pedigree but on services rendered. The great person is a big brother or big sister to the world. No person is born great nor has greatness thrust upon him or her but must achieve it. Thus in a land of titles, a nobleman may not be great, while a commoner is.

All greatness is unconscious, or it is little and naught.

—THOMAS CARLYLE

But he that is greatest among you shall be your servant.

—MATTHEW 23:11

More Than Parrotism

T he person who has been given a keen, intelligent mind has the potential for noteworthy achievement. But this alone is not the whole story.

More must be said. For one can have a head full of brains and still be woefully lacking in judgment and practicality. This is why some educated people have so little sense. They have intelligent ignorance. Consequently, nearly everything they run—though their I.Q. is high—is run into the ground. In parrotism their score is high, but in intellectual wisdom it's very low.

Much learning does not teach a man intelligence.
—HERACLITUS
(540-480 B.C.)

Great men are not always wise....
—JOB 32:9

Blessed With Health

Our most valuable wealth is good health. Without it, stocks, bonds, lands, oil wells and gold mines are of little value.

We can catch disease but not health. Health is something to pursue and maintain. To obtain it, there are rules to follow. What we put into the body, how we work and how we rest, and how we handle our emotions make for health or destroy it. If we perfectly followed the rules of health, beginning in childhood, we could greatly reduce the size of the medical profession.

Yes, we need to be concerned about our health, but not to the point we can't enjoy it.

Health is the second blessing that we mortals are capable of; a blessing that money cannot buy.

—Izzak Walton

A merry heart doeth good like a medicine....
—Proverbs 17:22

Personality

Why go against the grain in human relations when one can make it easier? Of course, it is difficult to manifest a winsome personality if a great character does not exist. It is hard to show a loving spirit when love is lacking, and consideration when selfishness prevails, and helpfulness when empathy is wanting, and friendliness when only self is seen.

The heart is the center of personality, and thus by overhauling it one can alter his personality. Also, one should do a skin job on self—grow a skin the practical thickness. This will let him work happily and helpfully in spite of too many flowers from friends and too many brickbats from enemies.

In short, an attractive personality is one that attracts; and this is done by subordinating self for the good of others.

—ANONYMOUS

A good man out of the good treasure of the heart bringeth forth good things....

—MATTHEW 12:35

The Challenge of Capability

No person is capable of everything to the fullest. Hence he is not responsible for an ability he doesn't have or a demand he can't fulfill. But he is—definitely is—accountable for what he is capable of becoming, which is the real challenge of every life. However, most of us have only partially accepted the challenge of becoming and consequently don't know what we're capable of performing, for we have never pushed ourselves relentlessly enough to know.

Let us go our limit. That should be the high sight of all. Anything less is low aim and wasted ability.

The great law of culture is: Let each become all that he was created capable of being.
—THOMAS CARLYLE

...Lord, thou deliveredst unto me two talents: behold, I have gained two other talents beside them.
—MATTHEW 25:22

Fill Up or Fold Up

We have responsibilities that require attendance at various meetings. Eliminate attendance and many worthy endeavors would fold up. Stated in a nutshell, *fill up or fold up.*

Attendance! Church attendance! When people look at the CH??CH what do they see that is missing? UR. Why? When there is a pull of the world and a pull of the church, and the church loses, WHY? Simply stopping the leaks in attendance would in time overflow the auditorium.

Unfortunately, when it comes to church attendance, some people are "Every Day Absentists."
—ANONYMOUS

Not forsaking the assembling of ourselves together, as the manner of some is; but exhorting one another: and so much the more, as ye see the day approaching.
—HEBREWS 10:25

The Deeper You

Reason is vital, but so are feelings. Just to be made physically strong and scholarly great is not enough; that just might make us hard and insensitive. It is granted that we need a tough fiber, but we also need the ability to feel and to express those feelings. For he who works only from his head is merely a cold, calculating, intellectual machine.

In some experiences we find the intellect too heavy, and thus we need to go down into the emotional recesses of the heart and come up with something lighter. It is in the area of feeling—based on truth—that we find ourselves moved to loftier actions. So never be ashamed of your noble feelings; they are your deeper you.

To make others feel we must feel ourselves.
—BENJAMIN DISRAELI

And they said one to another, Did not our heart burn within us, while he talked with us by the way, and while he opened to us the scriptures?
—LUKE 24:32

Twice as Good

It is good to have something worthwhile to say, and it is just as good after it is said to stop. It is especially annoying when the speech is long and the thinking is short. Tediousness exasperates the listener, and repetition continues to weary him. Throwing a dictionary at him does not make him want to play ball with us.

In lengthy speech the main thought is apt to be lost; by the time the conclusion is reached, the beginning has been forgotten. This is why brevity has been called "the soul of wit."

Good things, when short, are twice as good.
—GRACIAN

But when ye pray, use not vain repetitions, as the heathen do: for they think that they shall be heard for their much speaking.
—MATTHEW 6:7

What Delights Us?

It adds spark to personality to have a capacity for the delightful. It is truly a blessed people that delights in the right things, things that are clearly pointed out in the Bible and fully accepted by a refined society: upright people, just weights, true dealings, righteous lips, good reports, peace, another's fortune, clean fun, self-respect, children, knowledge of God's ways, offerings, prayer, and the law of the Lord.

Tell me the kind of things that bring you joy and I shall tell you the kind of person you are. For each is what he enjoys.

We can judge of a man by his delights and distastes.

—ANONYMOUS

But his delight is in the law of the Lord; and in his law doth he meditate day and night.

—PSALM 1:2

Flee From Evil

Evil—it even sounds bad. It is bad! The fruit of evil comes from evil roots. But it is remediable. Just striking at the branches, however, will not cure it. If we would relieve ourselves and the world of it, we must strike at its roots. The strike is easier made when one understands the deceptive nature of evil, for this lessens the enticement of it. Though it builds, it never lasts. It triumphs for a time but never conquers. It offers success but gives failure. It holds out joy but dishes out sorrow. It is the great deceiver! And expediency does not make it right nor alter the law of reaping what is sown.

By all means flee from it. If we play with evil, it becomes more playful. But if we shun it, it shuns us.

Avoid the evil and it will avoid thee.
—GERMAN PROVERB

Abhor that which is evil; cleave to that which is good.
—ROMANS 12:9

Contagious Courtesy

Courtesy is the universal language understood the world over. It gives its possessor passport to every hamlet, town and city round the globe. It opens doors and hearts. Politeness twice blesses— blesses him who gives it and him who receives it. The rewards are invaluable, and the cost is nothing.

It thinks considerately, speaks thoughtfully, listens patiently, and thus lubricates the wheels of friction in a grinding society. It shows civility and culture. Moreover, it is contagious. More people need to be exposed. It needs to spread.

We cannot always oblige, but we can always speak obligingly.

—VOLTAIRE

And Julius courteously entreated Paul....

—ACTS 27:3

Slaves to Fashion

F ashion is a tyrant that says, *Unless you follow me you are a nobody.* Consequently, fashion gets rid of more clothes than use wears out. The latest fashion may or may not be the wisest, for oftentimes it is inspired only by a desire for change and newness with no regard for adequacy, beauty, modesty or expense.

While some ridicule the prevailing craze, they slavishly obey it. What a master! Isn't it strange that we laugh at old fashions (seen in pictures) when in just a few years we shall laugh at the present ones? We do not want to admit that we are fickle, but we must admit that fashion is. The pictures prove it.

Fashion is something barbarous, for it produces innovation without reason and imitation without benefit.

—GEORGE SANTAYANA

Do ye look on things after the outward appearance?

—II CORINTHIANS 10:7

No Use to Grumble

An Old Testament scripture says, "And when the people complained, it displeased the Lord." No wonder! For it is not pleasant to God, man or beast. It lacks understanding and tolerance.

Now for those of us who get grumbled at, it will not hurt us unless we let it. Obviously the grumbler has a chip on his shoulder, and we can avoid knocking it off by patting him on the back. We may have to look long and hard to find something praiseworthy, but the best way to fight evil is with good.

It hain't no use to grumble and complain,
*   It's jest as easy to rejoice;*
When God sorts out the weather and sends rain,
*   Why rain's my choice.*

—JAMES WHITCOMB RILEY

There are murmurers, complainers, walking after their own lusts; and their mouth speaketh great swelling words....

—JUDE 16

We Can All Be Patriots

As long as our country has "a government of the people, by the people, and for the people," then our looking out for our country is actually looking out for ourselves. Indeed, patriotism is a vital condition of both national and personal security.

But blind patriotism is no real patriotism at all, just sanctified loyalty gone mad. So I would never say, "My country right or wrong," but would rather say, "My country when right, keep it right; when wrong, set it right." That's true patriotism. It builds a country worth building and keeps a country worth keeping. It puts together the elements of a civilized heritage worthy to be transmitted to our children.

We can't all be Washingtons but we can all be patriots and behave ourselves in a human and Christian manner.

—CHARLES L. BROWNE

Then the chief captain came, and said unto him, Tell me, art thou a Roman? He said, Yea.

—ACTS 22:27

Meet Luck Halfway

A lean, ragged, forlorn man, sitting on the curb, moaned, "I ain't never had any luck." Could it be because he never liked work, diligence, thrift, self-preservation or challenge? Ordinarily, luck is something we make for ourselves. The harder we work, the more fortune favors us. The more diligent we are, the luckier we get. The more wisdom we exercise, the more luck we have. Unquestionably, luck seems to be partial to efficiency.

Yes, I believe in the hand of God and that it is always inexplicably stretched out to us. His hand is a source of blessings. But that hand also points the way for us to follow if we would have a lucky break: "Labor that he may have." "Soweth that...he also reap." "Gather up the fragments." "Think." "Watch." These help luck along.

Diligence is the mother of good luck.
—BENJAMIN FRANKLIN

...seeing he giveth to all life, and breath, and all things.
—ACTS 17:25

Two Hearts in One

Love is the greatest thing in the world. So great that God is called love. So great that the First and Second Commandments are based upon it: First, love God; second, love neighbor. It is strong on unselfishness, kindness, sacrifice, tolerance, endurance, helpfulness and hope. Love doesn't make us all agree but does make us agreeable, doesn't dispel all anger but does give it a long fuse.

Affection makes a cottage more delightful than a mansion that doesn't have it and a biscuit tastier than a steak without it. Never asks for much. It can't be bought. Just gives itself away. Words can't express it. It's so great that if you can say how much you love, you love too little.

Two souls in one, two hearts in one heart.
—LATIN PROVERB

Many waters cannot quench love, neither can the floods drown it....
—SONG OF SOLOMON 8:7

Footshaking and Handshaking

Opportunity calls but is often found in making calls. As we open doors, we open possibilities. Human contact face to face does something that letters and telephone calls cannot accomplish. Shoe leather will trade in the marketplace. It can be swapped for friendship, alignment, support and greenbacks. Handshaking is magnetic and warm, encourages togetherness. But first and beyond that, something else is needed: footshaking.

The churches, businesses and other establishments that do well are strong on footshaking, another word for *visitation*. And as we open doors, let us conduct ourselves in such a way that we don't close them behind us.

It was a delightful visit—perfect, in being much too short.

—JANE AUSTEN

And some days after Paul said unto Barnabas, Let us go again and visit our brethren....

—ACTS 15:36

What Is Unhappiness?

What is it?

It's wanting something and then making ourselves miserable to get it. It's a biting conscience from the teeth of yesterday's ghosts. It's a loneliness that comes from too much self in the heart which leaves too little room for others. It's a depreciation of self, which makes it hard to live with self. It's an intolerance of others, which frustrates associations. It's life devoid of gripping goals to give it challenge and zest, just drifting. It's envy, jealousy, hate, unforgiveness, the unrelenting tormentors of man. It's the reaping of wild oats that won't nourish. It's nothing to do but to run around and have a good time, which soon loses its appeal. It's life without meaning, no commitment to God to breathe substance into it.

Finally, it's something to overcome!

Whoever does not regard what he has as most ample wealth is unhappy, though he be master of the world.

—EPICURUS
(341-270 B.C.)

...therefore the misery of man is great upon him.
—ECCLESIASTES 8:6

Hands of Charity

C harity is supplying the needs of those in want. Its source is found in an attitude. The outstretched hands of charity are directed by a big, unselfish heart.

While "charity begins at home," the big heart won't let it stay there. It feels with others, puts itself in their place, and moves accordingly. It is the Golden Rule in practice: "Therefore all things whatsoever ye would that men should do to you, do ye even so to them."

Of course, giving bread to a person is not as helpful as giving aid and direction to earn it. Give him a loaf and he eats it; but give him the know-how and opportunity to earn it, and after he has eaten it he can earn another one.

Charity gives itself rich; covetousness hoards itself poor.

—GERMAN PROVERB

Blessed is he that considereth the poor: the Lord will deliver him in time of trouble.

—PSALM 41:1

A Child's Copybook

Parents—what an extensive and heavy responsibility! Because a parent's influence is a child's copybook.

If we want our children to be honest, be honest. If we want them to be truthful, be truthful; never let them hear us tell a lie. If we want them to be sensitive to the needs of others, let them see us help the sick, destitute and downtrodden. If we want to guard them from becoming alcoholics, don't drink before them. If we want them to be self-supporting, teach them to work. If we want them to be law-abiding, demand obedience. And if we want them to go to church, take them. They learn from us.

Parents wonder why the streams are bitter when they themselves have poisoned the fountain.
—JOHN LOCKE

And he did that which was right in the sight of the Lord, and walked in the ways of David his father, and declined neither to the right hand, nor to the left.
—II CHRONICLES 34:2

Good Manners

Good manners make sense. Insensitivity toward others does not. Good manners may be called subservient, but they are the kind that give mastery. For they lubricate the wheels of society and let one operate as the master of the situation. The person of refined manners has more concern for the feelings of others than for the expression of his own, more care for the people at the table than for the food, more interest in those standing than in his own comfort, and more concern for the losers in a game than in running up an unnecessary, humiliating score.

Good breeding never overeats, over-talks, over-steps, over-presses, or overstays. But it can overlook the bad manners of others and often has to do this.

Some people's manners would shock a monkey.
—AMERICAN ADAGE

And they spake unto him, saying, If thou be kind to this people, and please them, and speak good words to them, they will be thy servants for ever.
—II CHRONICLES 10:7

True Eloquence

The secret of eloquence is understanding and truth. Unless the message is understood, it is worthless; and unless it is the truth, it is not worth telling. Of course, any speech is dull if the hearer is. Better ears make better tongues and vice versa. The truest and sublimest eloquence is brief (for examples, the Lord's Prayer and the Gettysburg Address). But more needs to be said. Eloquence needs a subject, an occasion, and a man behind it. It is noteworthy that the most eloquent communicators have high-pointed their addresses with words and phrases from the Bible. Its profundity, simplicity, directness and beauty give it a superior rhetoric.

Foot and a half long words are not eloquent.
—ADAPTED, HORACE
(65-8 B.C.)

A word fitly spoken is like apples of gold in pictures of silver.
—PROVERBS 25:11

Fig Leaves

People have been concerned with apparel ever since Adam and Eve sewed fig leaves together and made themselves aprons. Clothes do talk, and a lack of them also talks.

While clothes do not make the man, they do cover man and make him more acceptable. Unquestionably, good clothes are no substitute for a threadbare soul, but they are appealing. Fine feathers do not make fine birds, but they do make them more attractive.

The best dressed are not overdressed nor underdressed, but comely—nor necessarily costly—and above all, modestly covered.

Plain without pomp, rich without show.
—JOHN DRYDEN

In like manner also, that women adorn themselves in modest apparel....
—I TIMOTHY 2:9

Our Use of the Past

The past—good or bad—can be hurtful or helpful, depending on the use that's made of it. If it's used to rest on, it's unproductive; but if it's used as a foundation, it can be the basis for higher achievements.

If we were mistreated in the past, if unforgiven, it can make today grudge-bearing; but if forgiven and forgotten, we can live today free and unweighted down. If our past is marked with wrong decisions and poor shots, learn from it. There is no better teacher. If our past is marred with sin, it can be self-destructive and conscience-hurting; but if forgiven, it is the turning point in a new, vibrant life. Let us make our past our friend—not an enemy. We are not required to live the past. We can put it behind us. Today is our day.

We ought not to look back unless it is to derive useful lessons from past errors, and for the purpose of profiting by dear bought experience.
—GEORGE WASHINGTON

Oh that I were as in months past, as in the days when God preserved me....
—JOB 29:2

Bend or Break

Maladjustment gives an inflexibility that breaks under stress, but adjustment bends and survives unbroken. What should be changed and can be changed, change it; what can't, accept it. In the spring and fall we have time changes. Some do not like it; but by freely adapting to the change, it is easier.

The best of plans sometimes go awry. We are constantly met with changing circumstances, which demand adaptation. If your alarm clock fails, reconcile yourself to a shorter day. If your health fails, learn to stay in bed for awhile. If son or daughter goes off to college or marries, reconcile to the loneliness. If your ship doesn't come in, adjust to the disappointment and send another one out. This is not depressing. This is the means of overcoming what causes depression.

Every adaptation is a noble victory—a victory over a disappointed self. This is practical. This is heroic.

A hand that closes never to open again is useless.
—General Douglas MacArthur

For though I be free from all men, yet have I made myself servant unto all, that I might gain the more.
—I Corinthians 9:19

A Little Folly

Here are some of the many ways folly shows itself: Acts wiser than it is. Is hasty of spirit. Bites and devours one another. Shuts the stable door after the horse is stolen. Uses its tongue to cut its own throat. Refuses the learning of the wise. Tries to live in a fool's paradise. Acts without thinking, which can cost both money and life. For instance, lighting a match to see if there is gas in the car usually proves there is.

At times we are all a little foolish, but with sober thinking and God's help we can lessen it. And just to look at others can be of help.

Folly in all of every age we see,
The only difference lies in the degree.
—Nicolas Boileau-Despreaux

This their way is their folly....

—Psalm 49:13

Pay Every Debt

It has been said, "We get what we pay for." Now let's be sure we pay for it. However, the debt-riders say, "Oh, don't worry, the creditor can't take it with him anyway." Neither can the payless debtor, but he still has an obligation to pay his bills.

One of the deepest principles of religion is the honesty that is seen in the payment of debts. It won't do a person any good to go to church and sit in the amen corner if his unpaid bills are stacked so high he can't see God. Though the debtor never pays, he never fails to make excuses; but excuses don't settle defaults. When payments are due, God speed us on time. Another thing—he who pays can always borrow.

Wilt thou seal up the avenues of ill?
Pay every debt, as if God wrote the bill.
—RALPH WALDO EMERSON

The wicked borroweth, and payeth not again....
—PSALM 37:21

Let Peace Prevail

Some make peace. Some make strife. Some make neither. The latter is true of those in the cemetery: They neither cause trouble nor throw oil on troubled waters. But who wants to be a corpse?

It is impossible for one to be at peace with others if he is at war with himself. The reason Cain had trouble with Abel was that Cain had trouble with Cain. As seen in Abel's life, freedom from combativeness is not always the same as peace. We can refrain from fighting, but it does not always keep the other fellow from knocking us down. However, one thing all of us can do is "follow after the things which make for peace," and this is a blessed estate.

Peace is the fairest form of happiness.
—WILLIAM ELLERY CHANNING

Blessed are the peacemakers: for they shall be called the children of God.
—MATTHEW 5:9

Life's Blueprint

Only those who are good at planning are good at succeeding. No plans, no fulfillment. Nothing is more ineffective than unplanned activity—motion but no direction, movement but no goal. Ships don't make the harbor by drifting. Neither do human lives aimlessly land in the harbor of accomplishment.

Look at a great life; it was planned achievement. Plans are the blueprint for the house we build called life. Every wise builder has blueprints that he carries out in a systematic way. Decide what you want to do with your life. Have a definite plan, and then piece by piece nail it together.

When a man does not know what harbor he is making for, no wind is the right wind.

—SENECA
(8 B.C.-A.D. 65)

I thought on my ways, and turned my feet unto thy testimonies.

—PSALM 119:59

Crowning Gift

He is not wise who butts his head against reason, for reason stands and the head is bruised. This is why humans tumble and nations crumble: Reason goes unheard, and rashness shouts to its victims. One word brings so many woes: impulse. Indeed, impulse sometimes pays off, but only when it's in keeping with reason.

Devoid of reason, we live like animals; for the ability to reason is what distinguishes us from the lower creatures. Dogs and cats keep on living the same way, but we through the process of reason improve our lot. At times we all go astray, but reason can cut down the failures. Think. Analyze. Compare. Calculate. Project. It is our heritage, our privilege and our safeguard.

Reason is God's crowning gift to man.
—WILLIAM SHAKESPEARE

Come now, and let us reason together, saith the Lord....
—ISAIAH 1:18

Grasshopper Syndrome

Pessimism, simply put, is just a sophisticated word for no faith or little faith. Weak nerves may call it safety first, but it's not safe to be too scared ever to move or too afraid ever to see a challenge.

The pessimist doesn't like: *Sunshine*—it squints the eyes, or *rain*—it washes the soil. *Knowledge*—it increases responsibility, or *ignorance*—it stifles opportunity. *Smiles*—they pucker the cheeks, *or frowns*—they wrinkle the face. *Health*—it demands more of a person, or *illness*—it hinders accomplishment. *Fun*—says it won't last, or *languor*—afraid it will last. Concerning any good proposal, the pessimist thinks it can't be done.

The optimist proclaims that we live in the best of all possible worlds; and the pessimist fears this is true.

—JAMES BRANCH CABELL

...and we were in our own sight as grasshoppers, and so we were in their sight.

—NUMBERS 13:33

Kinship Stronger Than Blood

Kinsfolk—this is something nearly everybody has. And while we may feel free to criticize them, we do not want the other fellow to do it. And when others do, we are apt to bristle and join hands against the attack. This is neither all good nor all bad. At worst, it shows blind loyalty. At best, it shows family attachment.

Thanks be to God, not all relatives are alike. The kin is the same, but the kind is different. Lineage doesn't always line us up the same. In a broader sense, the recognition of a common parentage—Adam and Eve—makes the whole world kin. And in another sense, common faith, common love, common interests and common goals give us a bond of kinship stronger than blood. It's heart relationship.

Fate chooses our relatives, we choose our friends.
—JACQUES DELILLE

And Naomi said unto her, The man is near of kin unto us, one of our next kinsmen.
—RUTH 2:20

Starving Our Fears

Fear sees ferocious lions that are only friendly kittens. Truly, one of the devastating enemies of man is fear. Just to fear a thing may be more painful than the thing itself because it is an emotion that feeds on itself and gets bigger with every feeding. It makes every problem bigger than it is and readily believes the worst. Let us learn to starve our hurtful fears, not feed them.

Splendid ideas, sound techniques and workable plans are paralyzed by fear. It prevents their starting; or if started, stops them before fruition. Of course, constructive fear is protective, like "fear God and keep his commandments." It's the destructive fear that hurts.

They can conquer who believe they can. He has not learned the first lesson of life who does not every day surmount a fear.
—RALPH WALDO EMERSON

For God hath not given us the spirit of fear; but of power, and of love, and of a sound mind.
—II TIMOTHY 1:7

Some Things Cannot Be Rushed

B e patient. Some things can't be rushed. Fretting and fuming won't make the sun rise any faster or go down any sooner. Patience—how we need it and how we often lose it. "Patience can remove mountains," but sometimes we get in too big a hurry and break the shovels and leave the mountain standing to mock us in our overly fast expectancy.

One of nature's secrets is patience—due process. Not even God made the world in a second or hour or day. One of the secrets of growth—physical, spiritual, material and educational—is patience. And one of the secrets of successful human relations is patience—forbearance. Be longsuffering. If we expect perfection, we ask for more than we can give.

All things come round to him who will but wait.
—HENRY WADSWORTH LONGFELLOW

Ye have heard of the patience of Job and have seen the end of the Lord; that the Lord is very pitiful, and of tender mercy.

—JAMES 5:11

Blessed Memory

 emory is our computer we plug into for tremendous benefits. It's our receptacle of knowledge (stores information), protector from harm (issues warnings), giver of wisdom (draws from experience), and supplier of joy (relives the happy moments). And a blessed moment that lives in memory shall never die.

To achieve happiness and success, some things should be remembered, other things forgotten. And it's tragic when the order is reversed. Blessed are those who can do both. Today we make tomorrow's memories. May they be sweet.

Oft in the stilly night,
Ere Slumber's chain has bound me,
Fond Memory brings the light
Of other days around me.

—THOMAS MOORE

When I call to remembrance the unfeigned faith that is in thee....

—II TIMOTHY 1:5

Reputation Is Important

While character—what we are—is priceless, reputation—what people think we are—is also valuable. Unquestionably, how we are perceived is an asset or a liability. A good reputation is first-rate business capital, an excellent calling card and a ready door-opener.

High standing may take years to reach but may be knocked down in a second, justly or unjustly. Though calumniators destroy reputation, they can't harm character. Yet their malicious tongues are injurious, for reputation—like china—is easily cracked and hard to mend. In such a case, the long view is needed; the defamer can sway earth, but he can't move heaven.

A good reputation is more valuable than money.
—PUBLILIUS SYRUS

...Timothy...was well reported of by the brethren that were at Lystra and Iconium.
—ACTS 16:1,2

Keep Growing

I f we want to be somebody tomorrow that we're not today, then we must grow. Really, that's what life is all about: growth. We were born to grow. And if we cease to grow, we start to die. As children we outgrew our clothes, and as adults we should outgrow the little spiritual garments that once covered smaller souls.

It is natural for every living thing to grow until it reaches the climax, and then the anti-climax comes. However, there is another kind of growth in which there should be no anti-climax— *spiritual growth* in which we get bigger and stronger with the passing of the years. Hence, there is no such thing as a finishing school; instead, the growth process is to continue.

Internal growth depends on what the soul is fed and the exercise of noble deeds.

— ANONYMOUS

...though our outward man perish, yet the inward man is renewed day by day.

—II CORINTHIANS 4:16

Sacred Ground

Reverence is an ennobling emotion, and only ignoble minds find it debasing. Man does not elevate his own littleness by trampling holy things. God is no joking matter. His name is not to be knocked around like a punching bag. For when we have been knocked out, He will still be in that bigger ring.

Let us, therefore, walk soberly and reverently in respect of God and that which pertains to Him. Most assuredly life has its comic situations that may be entered into with levity, but making fun of holy things is not funny. There are sacred grounds. Let's regard them as such.

Dear Lord and Father of mankind,
  Forgive our foolish ways!
Reclothe us in our rightful mind,
In purer lives Thy service find,
  In deeper reverence, praise.
                              —JOHN GREENLEAF WHITTIER

...holy and reverend is His name.
                              —PSALM 111:9

Scars Are Our Diplomas

L ife has its ups and downs, ecstasies and sufferings. While we don't like suffering, it surely has its compensations, otherwise the Wise Designer would not have permitted it in man's fate. It helps us to see if we are made of the right stuff and to really grasp the thought, "Man shall not live by bread alone." Trials and afflictions teach us the truth about our transitory state. Moreover, they produce a subdued patience, a humble temper, a kind disposition, an empathy toward other sufferers, and a recognition of higher priorities and more worthwhile values.

After passing through the rigors, though they cost a big price, we can often look back and see that they were beneficial. The scars are our diplomas.

The burden of suffering...is only the weight which is necessary to keep down the diver while he is hunting for pearls.
—JOHANN PAUL FRIEDRICH RICHTER

It is good for me that I have been afflicted; that I might learn thy statutes.
—PSALM 119:71

The Wings of Scandal

Scandal! Shame! And if the accused is famous, the shortcoming becomes special conversation, generates glee and spreads fast. For the scandal-mongers find more fun in circulating the faults of the mighty. It is the famous they especially like to pull down. Truly, heavy hangs the crown of prominence. But when evil words fly and scandal buzzes, there is this consolation (though small): It proves that the person is prominent; if not, the report would not have been so widely broadcast.

Even if the story is true and propriety was breached, we need to recognize that there is not anything so bad but that it gets worse by the telling. So let us not air it and add to its naughtiness. For we cannot raise ourselves by stepping on another who is down. Let us clip the wings of scandal.

That abominable tittle-tattle,
Which is the cud chewed by human cattle.
—LORD BYRON

Doth our law judge any man, before it hear him, and know what he doeth?
—JOHN 7:51

Opportunity in Overalls

Opportunity does not usually come labeled as such. Though it is there, it is seen only in proportion to our perception. This is why some people see it and others don't. There are no opportunities to closed eyes and deaf ears. Furthermore, opportunity is apt to come dressed in overalls, wearing working gloves, and this blinds some people.

If opportunity doesn't find us, let's find it. If we don't find it, let's make it. If there is no water, then dig a well. If the well doesn't flow, then pump it. Wake up! There are opportunities! The world is wide, and there is a place for each of us.

There is a tide in the affairs of men,
Which, taken at the flood, leads on to fortune.
—WILLIAM SHAKESPEARE

And truly, if they had been mindful...they might have had opportunity....
—HEBREWS 11:15

Alike but Different

By nature all men are alike. By environment, teaching and influence we become different. Whatever our problems are, nature is not at fault. For God is the author of nature, which obviously is much like God: must be obeyed, is impartial, is unswayed by passing fancies, gives to those who honor her, and is the source of knowledge.

Like God, nature is immutable. We don't conquer nature; we merely adapt ourselves to it. And necessity hastens the adaptation. The whole scope of nature needs to be considered. More specifically, any system that doesn't recognize man's human nature is wrought with impracticality and destined to failure.

In nature we recognize an infinite power.
—JOHANN WOLFGANG VON GOETHE

...the living God, which made heaven, and earth, and the sea, and all things that are therein.
—ACTS 14:15

What Is Progress?

What we call progression is often retrogression, wasted energy, costly nuisance. To make headway, the head must be used, at least somebody's.

Newness is not always progress. A thing isn't bad just because it's old—old breathing, old seeing, old hearing, old eating, old friends, old gospel. Neither is movement always progress, for one can move the wrong way. Right direction is required. Neither is change synonymous with progress, for a person can change from right to wrong and from truth to error. Neither is speed necessarily progress. It could be faster calamity.

Progress looks to end results. Giving a cannibal a knife and fork is not progress, but getting him to change his diet is. Progress is improvement!

The greater part of progress is the desire to progress.

—SENECA
(8 B.C.-A.D. 65)

I therefore so run, not as uncertainly; so fight I, not as one that beateth the air....

—I CORINTHIANS 9:26

Chain of Strong Thinks

P sychology is the science of mind and behavior. A thought makes a little groove in the mind that gets deeper with usage. It's like the ruts made by a car on a muddy road; usage makes them deeper. Moreover, it is easy for a car to head down the ruts, but it's hard to get it out. The same is true of the mind. Wake up in the morning, and the thinking heads for that easy groove. The remedy is to divert nerve-racking thinking into constructive thinking. Keep out of that devastating rut of "everything as usual," and finally the rut will vanish.

The world's greatest book on psychology is the Bible. It cleans up one's past, gives assurance of forgiveness, switches the thinking from self to others, lifts one when he stumbles, and inspires a higher reach. It gives a person something to live for because it has helped him to be a great somebody, a child of the King. A new mind created by new thinking!

A chain of thought is no stronger than its weakest think.

—ANONYMOUS

...for as he thinketh in his heart, so is he....

—PROVERBS 23:7

Good Neighbors

T he best part of good real estate is good neighbors. People make the biggest difference. This being true, the most expensive house set among vile persons is of little value.

Keeping your relationship with your neighbor on excellent terms is mutually helpful. Each can look out for the other. A good neighbor respects your property, your privacy, your time, lets you live in peace, and never keeps eyes that see nothing but you. Not nosey. Not envious. Not covetous. He is not too forward, yet is ever-ready to help when the need arises. Keep a good neighbor policy, which is easy when love calls the plays.

Love your neighbor, yet don't pull down your hedge.

—BENJAMIN FRANKLIN

...Thou shalt love thy neighbor as thyself.
—MATTHEW 22:39

With Wings as Eagles

There is no place between the cradle and the grave to quit. Life is a continuous struggle. There is but one real finishing school, life itself, and the diploma is a death certificate. There is only one thing worse than quitting, and that's to finish something that shouldn't have been started.

When things go wrong, as they sometimes will,
When the road you are trudging seems all uphill;
When the funds are low and the debts are high,
And you want to smile, but have to sigh;
When care is pressing you down a bit,
Rest if you must, but don't you quit.
You stick to the fight when you're hardest hit—
It's when things seem worst that you mustn't
  quit.

—Author Unknown

But they that wait upon the Lord shall renew their strength; they shall mount up with wings as eagles; they shall run, and not be weary; and they shall walk, and not faint.

—Isaiah 40:31

Read and Grow

Reading lets us walk down the avenues of another's mind. It's a quick way to learn what it took the author years to experience and grasp.

The ability to read is an accomplishment, but the person who can read and doesn't has no advantage over the person who can't read. And if he does read, it's still not to his advantage unless the materials are helpful. It won't fill blank heads to read what blockheads write. Reading worthless materials is like going to a table that has no food.

As we read, we think; and as we think, we become. Therefore, a little constructive reading every day will put us ahead of those who don't.

Show me a family of readers, and I will show you the people who move the world.

—Napoleon

Till I come, give attendance to reading....

—I Timothy 4:13

Pleasant Guests

Here are a half dozen don'ts for guests to follow:
(1) Don't invade when not invited. (2) Don't exploit
the host and run up the bill. (3) Don't take over; it
is somebody else's home or party. (4) Don't embar-
rass the host by making comparisons. (5) Don't
stay long enough to weary the host. (6) Don't
always be a guest and never a host.

And here are a half dozen do's: (1) Be grateful.
(2) Be polite. (3) Make the host feel comfortable.
(4) Add to the spirit of the occasion. (5) Always
remember that you are there because of another's
hospitality. (6) Be reciprocative.

What is pleasanter than the tie of host and guest?
—AESCHYLUS
(525-456 B.C.)

If any of them that believe not bid you to a feast,
and ye be disposed to go; whatsoever is set before
you, eat, asking no question for conscience sake.
—I CORINTHIANS 10:27

A Time for Humor

Just think what life would be like if there were no humor, just one long stay in the morgue. Jesus occasionally spiced His teachings with a little humor, like "strain at a gnat and swallow a camel."

People are greatly disagreed on humor. What is funny to one may not tickle another's funny bone. The highest humor is not off-color, dirty, or at the expense of somebody else. The ability to see the funny side can ease tension, calm nerves and quicken insight to problems.

While not everybody has a sense of humor, nobody wishes to admit that he does not have it.

Ah, but a man's clear gravity should at times be mixed with clean wit.

—ANONYMOUS

A time to weep, and a time to laugh....

—ECCLESIASTES 3:4

The Right of Opinion

E very person has the right to his own opinion, even if it disagrees with mine. And in the honest and respectful exchange of opinions, I may change his or he may change mine. This dialogue on opposing views can be enlightening and the means of promoting unity.

However, opinions—even the agreement on opinions—do not determine the right of a matter. Our opinions about the time of day don't change the clock of the universe. Neither does our opinion of the weather turn back the clouds. So our chief concern should be to be right—not necessarily consistent, but right, which lends itself to hearing another's viewpoint.

The foolish and the dead alone never change their opinion.

—JAMES RUSSELL LOWELL

I said I will answer also my part; I also will show mine opinion.

—JOB 32:17

Not the Only Pebble

One of man's greatest needs is to take his eyes off self and focus them on others. See another's viewpoint; he might be right. At least give him a hearing. See the man who limps; he may have a tack in his shoe that's not easily removed. See the lonely person who longs for notice; a friendly word can be a healing balm for a forlorn heart. See the sick person who struggles between life and death; he is apt to appreciate our prayers. See the discouraged person whose world has fallen apart; our lift can raise him from despair to a new effort. See the person entangled in the web of sin; he needs our help.

And in helping others, we help ourselves.

You're not the only pebble on the beach.

—HARRY BRAISTED

For none of us liveth to himself, and no man dieth to himself.

—ROMANS 14:7

A God-Given Birthright

I t is man's God-given birthright to own possessions. Individual ownership motivates man and gives him a feeling of accomplishment, security and well-being.

Indeed, the Bible concept of man is one of freedom, internal and external. A man is free on the inside because he has something there he can call his own: his soul. Likewise, he is free on the outside because he has something there he can call his own: property. The possession of property is therefore only the outward manifestation of what a man possesses within: freedom, complete freedom.

I would rather sit on a pumpkin and have it all to myself than be crowded on a velvet cushion.
—HENRY DAVID THOREAU

Every man also to whom God hath given riches and wealth, and hath given him power to eat thereof, and to take his portion, and to rejoice in his labor; this is the gift of God.
—ECCLESIASTES 5:19

Walking in Another Man's Shoes

Since we are all brothers in adversity, then we should be all brothers in sympathy. It's the beating of two hearts alike because of the same impulse. It's mentally wearing another's shoes and drinking the bitter dregs of his cup. It's a high accomplishment, and it comes easier after we have suffered. When our tooth hurts, we have more pity toward our neighbor with a toothache.

While we are not to limp because of the cripple, we should extend help when it is needed. Sympathy without relief does not provide him any crutches. We need a sympathy that affects our own purse.

Sympathy, like ever other emotion, is meant to influence action. If it does not, what is the use of it?

—ALEXANDER MACLAREN

Then the Lord of that servant was moved with compassion, and loosed him, and forgave him the debt.

—MATTHEW 18:27

Vain Talk

There are some things about talk that are unproductive, even irritable: First, when it's untrue. Second, when it's exploitative. Third, when its untimely. Fourth, when it's uninteresting. Fifth, when it's impolite. Sixth, when it's too loud. Seventh, when it's whispered. Eighth, when it's too long. Ninth, when it says nothing. Talk has to come from somewhere—from a full mind or an empty head. If it comes from the latter, the only hope for it to stop is for the talker to close his mouth. And it's all right for him to say nothing provided he doesn't say it aloud and especially if he doesn't repeat himself. A course on How to Say Something is valuable, but one on How to Listen is priceless. The world likes a good talker but loves a good listener.

Discretion of speech is more than eloquence.
—FRANCIS BACON

For there are many...vain talkers....
—TITUS 1:10

On Bended Knee

One of the surest blessings for the sons and daughters of God is prayer. Its benefits are many and mighty: First, the fellowship of prayer with a holy God makes for holiness among the prayers. Second, it gives steadfastness; it is hard to stumble when we are on our knees. Third, it aids vision; the believer can see more on his knees than the unbeliever can see on tiptoe. Fourth, the bended knee produces courage—protects us from becoming weak-kneed. So when knees knock, kneel on them. Fifth, it taps the greatest power in the universe—Almighty God, who can do what we can't do.

For sure, God has the ability to answer prayer. We don't need proof. We need practice.

More things are wrought by prayer than this world dreams of.

—ALFRED LORD TENNYSON

For the eyes of the Lord are over the righteous, and his ears are open unto their prayers.

—I PETER 3:12

More Than a King

One of the musts of life is self-control. Without it, helplessness prevails and chaos rules. The person devoid of it is like a ship at sea with neither anchor nor rudder nor sail. This makes him unfit to live with self, all because he can't control self.

Self-mastery, how fundamental! How essential! So be in control. Control aims. Control thoughts. Control temper. Control lusts. Control appetites. Control extremes. Control discouragements. Some things are hard to handle, but it's not hard to control what we see, what we hear, what we read, where we go, and with whom we associate; and all five have a direct bearing on making stronger or weaker people.

He who reigns within himself and rules his passions, desires and fears, is more than a king.
—JOHN MILTON

But I keep under my body, and bring it into subjection....
—I CORINTHIANS 9:27

Defense Against Temptation

T emptation is one of the constant, threatening problems we have to deal with. But the kite has to face a similar problem of tricky winds and cross blows; that is, if it gets off the ground. Likewise, we rise higher from the temptation we resist, so every seductive situation is an opportunity to gain strength and ascend new heights.

But contrariwise, it is also a situation that can bring us down. Even the best of people have fallen, including the Apostle Peter. This being true, it certainly does not behoove those of us who have never walked in the shoes of a certain temptation to say how we would have stepped. Maybe we would have; maybe we wouldn't have. All need protection. The surest defense is to watch and pray and quote Scripture.

It is one thing to be tempted, another thing to fall.

—WILLIAM SHAKESPEARE

Watch and pray, that ye enter not into temptation: the spirit indeed is willing, but the flesh is weak.

—MATTHEW 26:41

Take Inventory of Self

Merchants take inventory to see where they stand, and every individual should do likewise. Each should look within. Examine your motives, your priorities, your concerns, your thoughts, your habits, your words and your deeds.

Ascertain the kind of man or woman you are. See yourself stripped of makeup and pretense. Ask yourself: Where have I succeeded? Where have I failed? Have I done my best? What is my view of life? How is it going to end? Be sincere. Be honest. It may be shocking, but it can be helpful. First know yourself, and then you can plan your program of self-improvement.

The life that is unexamined is not worth living.
—PLATO
(428-348 B.C.)

But let a man examine himself....
—I CORINTHIANS 11:28

Greatest Among You

The whole world stands in need of somebody to do something for somebody else. It is called *service*. The word is seen everywhere: on businesses, in advertisements and in mailouts. People want service—efficient service, honest service, quick service, friendly service. It attracts people.

Service is so appealing that the person who supplies it gets ahead of those who don't. It is so noteworthy that it is the means of exalting those who furnish it, even those in the kingdom of God, for the Bible states, "But he that is greatest among you shall be your servant." So let us give more thought to service than to remuneration, and the chances are the money will come later.

The highest of distinctions is the service of others.

—KING GEORGE VI

His lord said unto him, Well done, thou good and faithful servant....

—MATTHEW 25:21

Real Values

We can learn financial values and still impoverish ourselves by not knowing human values. It's the false estimate of values that brings the worst bankruptcy upon mankind: disappointment, distress and degradation.

There is no accurate appraisal of values unless they are measured by the happiness and betterment of mankind. The good old values—goodness, kindness, mercy, love, veracity, honesty, justice, conscience, loyalty and dependability—make their possessor rich even if his purse is empty. The richest are poor without them. What gives life real value is being something worthwhile and in having something dear to live for.

It is essential that the student acquire an understanding of and a lively feeling for values.... Otherwise he more closely resembles a well-trained dog than a harmoniously developed person.

—ALBERT EINSTEIN

For what is a man profited, if he shall gain the whole world, and lose his own soul?

—MATTHEW 16:26

Strutting Peacocks

Vanity is a strange, restless and benighted passion. It displays a pomp and splendor that would make a peacock feel second-rate. It sees its importance in everything—like the flea that rode the elephant across the bridge and later said, "We sure shook that bridge." It likes mirrors, can hardly pass one by. It thinks its copper is gold. It even brags about its vices.

It ever fishes for compliments, never fails to bait its hooks to pull them in. It is always hungry, never gets enough of the stuff on which it feeds. It wishes to be admired, but goes at it the repelling way. It brings on its own downfall, trips on itself. It is miserable, linked in the Bible to "vexation of spirit."

To be a man's own fool is bad enough; but the vain man is everybody's.
—WILLIAM PENN

...why then are ye thus altogether vain?
—JOB 27:12

Same Face Every Day

T he man of veracity is verily a man. Being an honorable man, he does not need to wear the fig leaves of deceit to hide the naked truth. His heart beats in tune with facts. His every fiber is one of honesty. He wears the same face every day. It is not hard for him to speak the truth, for he has truth on the tip of his tongue; and he has it there because he has it at the root of his tongue. He is true.

It is hard to believe a person is telling the truth if you believe that you would lie in the same circumstances. So if a report is not believed, it could be as much the fault of the listener as the communicator.

Press through:
Nothing can harm if you are true.
—EDWIN MARKHAM

A faithful witness will not lie: but a false witness will utter lies.
—PROVERBS 14:5

When School Is Out

The smallest acorn shows there is no death; just plant it. The burst of spring with a thousand marvels is too much for us not to believe that "this mortal must put on immortality." And when it occurs, "death is swallowed up in victory." Death is the transition that allows a person to go from this world into another one.

Death is a wise plan. Life on earth is too undeveloped, too unfinished, and ends too short of the highest aspirations and noblest dreams. It is meant to be only a schooling. Can the schooling be in vain? No! And when school is out, we go home. This gives permanence to the Creator's work and keeps it from ending in failure. It makes sense!

Dust thou art, to dust returnest,
Was not spoken of the soul
—HENRY WADSWORTH LONGFELLOW

Then shall the dust return to the earth as it was: and the spirit shall return unto God who gave it.
—ECCLESIASTES 12:7

Eyes That See

What we see and exalt in our minds becomes the molder of our lives and the shaper of our days. Indeed, what we see has great bearing on where we go.

Some people never ascend the higher ground because they never see the mountain peak. They languish in the dried, dusty plains below. There are wonderful advancements, blessed attainments, lucrative opportunities and glorious occasions that call, but they don't exist for some because they do not have the vision to discern them. Eyes that do not see!

The greatest vision sees not only the events of today, but foresees their effects on tomorrow. Eyes that see!

Who saw life steadily and saw it whole.
—MATTHEW ARNOLD

Where there is no vision, the people perish....
—PROVERBS 29:18

Fire of Enthusiasm

There is no substitute for brains; but if there could be, it would be *enthusiasm*. It is a genius all its own. It grips the heart, spurs the effort, and makes duty a pleasure; and without it, powerful thoughts are useless. It takes fire to make the pot boil.

Fervency is unmistakable evidence that a person is fully sold on what he's doing, which is very vital. For the fire we would kindle in others must first burn in ourselves. Indeed, the story of achievement is the story of the burning heart. Be enthusiastic. The secret is to give yourself.

Enthusiasm is the mother of effort, and without it nothing great was ever accomplished.
—RALPH WALDO EMERSON

So then because thou art lukewarm, and neither cold nor hot, I will spew thee out of my mouth.
—REVELATION 3:16

A Blameless Life

He is all fault who says he has never been at fault. Humanity is frailer than that. If you have never erred, you are only a manikin fit for a store window, which is far different from the world where people really live and actually wrestle with temptation. There the highest calling and the noblest accomplishment is to be blameless.

We are not angels. We cannot wear white garments never soiled, but with God's grace they can be cleaned and we can live blameless lives—lives in which the ought against us has been reconciled. Especially the person who holds a position of trust in either church or government or school or business should be blameless. Concerning the church, the Bible specifies it. The people are entitled to confidence.

Wearing the white flower of a blameless life.
—ALFRED LORD TENNYSON

Giving no offense in anything, that the ministry be not blamed....
—II CORINTHIANS 6:3

A Gibraltar

When the future of our country, or the welfare of our people, or the purity of the church, or the prosperity of anything precious is at stake, we must be undaunted! Unmoved! A Gibraltar! Not shifting sands!

Let us remain firm in our beliefs as we face the calls of popularity, the harangues of horrendous hordes, the inducements of temporary gain, the lusts for power, the threats of avengers, the smears of reputation killers, the summons of blind leaders, and the intimidations of villains in high places.

Is popularity so appealing, promotion so precious, temporary gain so good, and silence so golden as to be purchased at the price of selling our convictions? Forbid it! We must hold to our convictions to be our real selves. This is essential, absolutely essential, if we would be heroes in the world's struggles.

To be weak is to be miserable.

—JOHN MILTON

Stand fast in one spirit, with one mind.

—PHILIPPIANS 1:27

Rest for the Weary

L ife has its weariness. What man has done to harm himself! He has turned the earth into a jungle of weariness. In contrast, heaven is described as a place where "the weary be at rest."

But you can cut down earth's weariness with proper care: Keep work and play in balance. Refresh yourself by feeding your soul. Do not expect too much of yourself and of others. Take time; after all, the earth was not made in a day. Do not push yourself too hard. Look ahead. Seek the presence of cheerful people. And cast unbearable burdens on the Lord. Let common sense be your teacher. All of this is refreshing. If every flower enjoys the air it breathes, not wearied beyond its tolerance, then so should you! And so should I!

O bed! O bed! delicious bed!
That heaven upon earth to the weary head.
—THOMAS HOOD

And the king, and all the people that were with him, came weary, and refreshed themselves there.
—II SAMUEL 16:14

Overpriced Living

There are some life styles that we cannot afford. The penalties are too high. Where there is no abstinence there is the wreckage of broken lives, broken families, broken friendships, broken purses and broken dreams.

How can anything be enjoyable and satisfying that wrecks health, shortens life, destroys marriage, loses respect, cuts off employment, and possibly endangers the soul? It's as simple as this: Abstain and gain, or dissipate and destroy.

Refrain tonight;
And that shall lend a kind of easiness
To the next abstinence: the next more easy;
For use almost can change the stamp of nature.
—WILLIAM SHAKESPEARE

Abstain from all appearance of evil.
—I THESSALONIANS 5:22

A Problem World

So we have problems. This is a problem world. Show me a person with no earthly difficulties, and you will have to show me one that is dead. Our stay on earth is beset with troubles, and we must meet them.

This is the way to handle them: First, seek God's help and take counsel from Him. Second, recognize each problem as it begins to appear and solve it by cutting it off before it gets started. Third, approach the trying situation with wisdom and calmness. Fourth, think. Rashness creates problems, thinking unravels them. Fifth, some problems defy one-hundred-percent solution. In such cases, live with them, adjust to them, and then they are not such burdens after all.

It is difficulties that show what men are.
—EPICTETUS
(A.D. 50-120)

...we went through fire and through water: but thou broughtest us out into a wealthy place.
—PSALM 66:12

Doing What Is Right

Whether to go with the right or the wrong is an ever-pressing decision for man. Each beckons, and the decision that is made affects destiny. Though the world is filled with many wrongs supported by many people, it's still my firm conviction that nearly everybody deep down in his heart wants to do right.

The major problems are a lack of knowledge or a temporary temptation that sways him to the wrong. Sometimes it's peer pressure. Clearly it's not a matter of who is right but what is right. So let us follow the straight course even if we have none to walk with us but God.

A man in the right with God on his side is in the majority.

—HENRY WARD BEECHER

And thou shalt do that which is right and good in the sight of the Lord....

—DEUTERONOMY 6:18

Keep on Shooting

P erfection is something to shoot at but not with a single-barrel shotgun. We need a repeater rifle. And with such, though we miss the mark, we can keep on shooting at it.

This is the paradox: No one can be perfect unless he admits his faults; but if he does, he's not perfect.

Perfection never built a church, established a home, ran a business, or upheld a nation. But striving for it has helped. We never make improvement without trying. If we're imperfect after trying, think how much worse we would be if we didn't. It does help. Keep it up!

The indefatigable pursuit of an unattainable perfection, even though it consists in nothing more than in the pounding of an old piano, is what alone gives a meaning to our life on this unavailing star.

—Logan Pearsall Smith

Be ye therefore perfect, even as your Father which is in heaven is perfect.

—Matthew 5:48

Let Us Worship

Worship evidently comes naturally, for in every inhabitable part of the earth, near and far, people are inclined to worship. This is understandable. For man—spirit as well as flesh—has a longing to be in communion with the Great Spirit.

In our country, we have the freedom to worship and the freedom not to worship. However, the latter stifles the spirit and sets man on a beastly course that slowly but surely destroys all freedoms.

Worship should be "in spirit and in truth," regulated by truth and from man's spirit, devoid of any ulterior motive and free of any financial gain. He who goes to worship for a price would worship the devil too, if the price gets higher.

Man cannot live all to this world. If he worship not the true God, he will have his idols.
—THEODORE PARKER

O come, let us worship and bow down.....
—PSALM 95:6

Served by Riches

Riches within themselves are neither good nor bad but can be made into either, depending upon how they are perceived and held. If they are loved, they are the root of all evil. If they command, they make slaves. If they are unused, they are worthless. If they change one's only view of success into $UCCE$$, they are devastating. If they are regarded as the answer to all of our needs, they are deceptive and will mock us on our deathbeds.

On the other hand, if riches are viewed as a supplier of necessities, a safeguard against poverty, a protector from beggary, an aid in old age, and a means of helping others and good causes, they are truly a ready convenience and a great blessing.

Wealth is a good servant, a very bad mistress.
—FRANCIS BACON

...God, who giveth us richly all things to enjoy....
—I TIMOTHY 6:17

The Genius of Perseverance

Perseverance wins the race—if it's long enough. This is why the tortoise came in ahead of the rabbit: continuance. And this is why the mighty oak was felled: Little strokes stayed with the job.

Indeed, success doesn't come magically, easily or free of setbacks. Failure comes occasionally, but successful people don't give up. They're not fainthearted. They're not beaten. They're not quitters. When they suffer a setback, they make a comeback by going on. Accordingly, we must say that perseverance is a kind of genius—a kind that makes a big difference between failure and success. To end well, we must finish the task.

The slogan "Press on" has solved and always will solve the problems of the human race.
—CALVIN COOLIDGE

Behold, we count them happy which endure.
—JAMES 5:11

A Cause of Contempt

I t is helpful for friends to be close but not too close, for it is possible to get so close that it leaves no room for the friend's life to take shape individually.

Most people like company but not all the time. Though your visit is as sweet as honey, too much of it can be loathsome. While it is supportive to hold another's hand, it is also helpful to turn it loose. Too much presence can make another's heart grow fonder of your absence.

Moderation is very necessary in human relations. When a woman sticks out her hand, she may not necessarily want it kissed.

Familiarity breeds contempt.

—AESOP
(C. 550 B.C.)

My kinsfolk have failed, and my familiar friends have forgotten me.

—JOB 19:14

The Real Winner

He who wins isn't always the winner, and he who loses isn't always the loser. Victory goes beyond subjection or the highest tally: (1) Victory for plaudits instead of peace is no victory. Let the victor take the laurels, but let him give his love. "Love thine enemy." (2) Triumph that is easy hardly makes the conqueror a hero; the match is too uneven. (3) Mastery won on perversions or half-lies or cheating doesn't make a champion. In time the cheers will turn to jeers.

Now in the behalf of the tagged loser: (1) He who is a good loser is a winner—a victor over childishness. (2) He who learns from his mistakes is a victor. He will be ready and smarter next time. And (3) he who conquers self is a conqueror. Of all the world's victories, this is the greatest.

Victory is a thing of the will.

—MARSHALL FOCH

...Let us go up at once, and possess it; for we are well able to overcome it.

—NUMBERS 13:30

Just People

We are just people, come from the same ancestry, made of the same clay. No common people. No uncommon people. Just people. Errant people. Nevertheless, each of us is sacred, made in God's image, and is the object of God's love, fitted and equipped to have dominion over the earth.

Give the people the facts, and they (the majority) will make the right decisions. Ordinarily they respond to us like we treat them. We find in them what we bring. We get from them what we give. And we love them not so much for what they've done for us as for what we've done for them.

Whatever you may be sure of, be sure of this,
that you are dreadfully like other people.
—OLIVER WENDELL HOLMES

And hath made of one blood all nations of men for to dwell on all the face of the earth....
—ACTS 17:26

Magnetic Friendliness

F riendliness is a magnetism that pulls people together though they are strangers. It notices, recognizes and acknowledges people, all of which people like. It vibrates with life and vitality that we prefer over a chunk of ice or a corpse.

Nearly everybody warms up when met with friendliness. Even a dog knows how to make friends, and he has never read a book on the topic. Friendliness is so valuable, yet it is free. Cultivate it to help others and ourselves. The charm of it will put welcome mats out for us and give us greater influence.

Yes, when I'm sour, friends are few,
When I'm friendly, folks are, too.
—ANONYMOUS

A man that hath friends must show himself friendly....
—PROVERBS 18:24

Life's Unknowns

L ife has its unknown and unplanned events that tax us: Breakdown of health. Accident. Death. Loss of job. Alienation of associates. False rumor. Betrayal. Trouble in the family. Waywardness of children. Disappointment. We just hadn't planned on it. Now we have to deal with it. And that too is life.

To successfully handle the problem, we need: (1) Courage—"be of good courage." (2) Prayer—"Nevertheless we made our prayer unto God." (3) A forgiving spirit—"Father, forgive them." (4) Faith and perseverance—"Though he slay me, yet will I trust in him." (5) Adjustment—"Can I bring him back again? I shall go to him, but he shall not return to me." Dire necessity adds strength by awakening the sleeping giant within us.

Behind the dim unknown,
Standeth God within the shadow, keeping
watch above his own.
—JAMES RUSSELL LOWELL

...thou knowest not what a day may bring forth.
—PROVERBS 27:1

Deal Gently With Another's Faults

F aults are human. This means we have lots of them because we are so human. They vary with people. We would have to be blind never to see any faults in the world, but we do not have to go around with a magnifying glass.

When we do see another's faults, never use them to berate him or to feel superior to him. Deal with his shortcomings as gently and patiently as with our own. Remember, any fault he has could have been our own. Concerning our own faults, face them and make a concerted effort to overcome them. We can. So, "press toward the mark."

Teach me to feel another's woe,
To hide the fault I see;
That mercy I to others show,
That mercy show to me.

—ALEXANDER POPE

With all lowliness and meekness, with long-suffering, forbearing one another in love.

—EPHESIANS 4:2

Stand Firm

T he unremitting, courageous spirit that stands firm can be described in one word: BACKBONE.

Be polite, courteous, kind, but firm. It is not bad to be firm, nor is it good to be goody-goody. To be a milquetoast is no accomplishment; all that is necessary is to be a pushover, devoid of either conviction or courage.

The wishy-washy, dilly-dally person will never go far because if he moves up, he later moves back. Without firmness all efforts fail. Even some preaching is not firm enough. People can't handle it because it's a little thick for a spoon and a little thin for a fork. Mush!

Real firmness is good for anything;
strut is good for nothing.
—ALEXANDER HAMILTON

Stand therefore, having your loins girt about with truth....
—EPHESIANS 6:14

Better Than Great Riches

A good name is very valuable: It leads to collateral at the bank, acceptance in the market, recommendation for a job and surety for relationships. An accused man with a good name is half freed, while an indicted man with a bad name is half hanged.

No matter which way the winds of fortune blow, as long as you maintain a good name you are rich. Though a person suffers name smear through no fault of his own—from calumniators— he is still rich if his character remains unblemished, for the character which built the name is more valuable than the name itself.

For my name and memory, I leave it to men's charitable speeches.

—FRANCIS BACON

A good name is rather to be chosen than great riches....

—PROVERBS 22:1

Assessed With Responsibilities

Just to live in the world assesses us with responsibilities. Every relationship, every connection, every commitment and every job makes us answerable. Responsibility, like the shadow, goes with us—even more so. For when the clouds come, the shadow vanishes but not responsibility; it is then more present than ever.

When duty beckons, irresponsibility shrugs and mumbles, "What is that to me?" but responsibility answers, "Here I come." So responsibility comes in proportion to demand and the ability to handle it, which is response to ability. And playing ostrich does not obliterate the obligation.

Responsibility walks hand in hand with capacity and power.

—J.G. HOLLAND

For unto whomsoever much is given, of him shall be much required....

—LUKE 12:48

Habits

Great is the power of habit, and use gives it an even stronger hold. Habit at first is just a cobweb but later becomes a cable.

The formation of personality and the destiny of life depend much on habits. We make the habits, and the habits make us; therefore, let us be sure we form good habits. Then the best in life will be just second nature with us.

Furthermore, we will not later have to go through the strenuous discipline of breaking them, for ridding ourselves of a habit is somewhat like peeling off the skin.

How use doth breed a habit in a man.
—WILLIAM SHAKESPEARE

...but ever follow that which is good, both among yourselves, and to all men.
—I THESSALONIANS 5:15

Smart Silence

There are times when silence is smart: First, when knowledge is lacking. Abraham Lincoln said, "Better to remain silent and be thought a fool, than to speak out and remove all doubt." Second, when we have nothing to say. Solomon said, "A prating fool shall fall." Third, when temper boils and wishes to blow off steam. James stated, "Behold, how great a matter a little fire kindleth: And the tongue is a fire, a world of iniquity." Fourth, when it's inviting to participate in gossip, for, as Solomon expressed it, "The words of a talebearer are as wounds." Fifth, when it will do no good. Jesus said that to speak when people won't listen is like casting "pearls before swine" who "trample them under their feet and turn again and rend you."

This means that ears can be smarter than tongues.

Silence at the proper season is wisdom, and better than any speech.

—PLUTARCH
(46-120 A.D.)

Whoso keepeth his mouth and his tongue, keepeth his soul from troubles.

—PROVERBS 21:23

Lifted by Praise

We get more done by praising than by blaming. Praise is excellent. It motivates and sounds mighty good—that is, unless it's for self. Then it sounds like a broken drum; it is out of tune with the music of public relations.

In praising others, we need to be open and sincere because left-handed praise is nothing but right-handed abuse. Furthermore, we should be discerning because not everybody is worthy of praise. Praising a fool only feeds his folly, and praising an incompetent only lifts him up for a fall.

Maybe a little satire is appropriate: If we are slow and short in giving praise now, just wait until the fellow dies. Too bad we wait until he can't read his tombstone.

We are all imbued with love of praise.
—LATIN PROVERB

As the fining pot for silver, and the furnace for gold; so is a man to his praise.
—PROVERBS 27:21

Avoiding Fools

There are many wise and Biblical reasons for keeping our distance from a fool. A fool (1) is devoid of wisdom, for "wisdom is too high for a fool." (2) He engages in mischief ("it is as sport to a fool to do mischief"). (3) He is given to wrath ("a fool's wrath is presently known"). (4) He is meddlesome ("every fool will be meddling"). (5) He has no restraint ("a fool uttereth all his mind"). (6) No one can tell him anything ("the way of a fool is right in his own eyes"). (7) And he is contentious ("a fool's lips enter into contention").

What is the ready conclusion? Steer away from him as much as possible.

Never argue with a fool; if you do, bystanders may not know which is which.

—ANONYMOUS

Go from the presence of a foolish man, when thou perceivest not in him the lips of knowledge.

—PROVERBS 14:7

Yes and No

One can say "Yes" without being a "Yes" person, just like he can say "No" without being a negative person or a routine objector. That which is good needs a "Yes" and that which is bad, a "No."

To know when to say "Yes" and when to say "No," however, is not always the simplest and the easiest to discern. When the decision is reached and the heart says "Yes," then let's say it like we mean it. But we need to be honest and flexible enough to reverse ourselves and to say "No" when we have more light that changes the color.

"Yes," I answered you last night;
  "No," this morning sir, I say:
Colors seen by candlelight
  Will not look the same by day.
                    —ELIZABETH BARRETT BROWNING

...let your yea be yea; and your nay, nay....
                    —JAMES 5:12

Profitable Exchange

T he good and successful life is a mixture of abandoning the bad and obtaining the good. This puts us in the age-old marketplace in which we buy something at the price of giving up something else. In giving up the wrong and its devastation, we gain the right and its invigoration. That has to be a profitable exchange.

In speaking of erroneous philosophies, bad habits and evil conduct, there is great triumph in one's being able to say, "Once I was...but now I'm different." That's one of the blessed qualities of man: We can improve. And that should be the challenge and goal of all.

When you have faults do not fear to abandon them.

—CONFUCIUS
(551-479 B.C.)

...put away the evil of your doings from before mine eyes; cease to do evil; learn to do well....
—ISAIAH 1:16,17

Finding Our Field

Three things need to be pointed out: First, where aptitude is lacking, one is limited in going high in certain, specific fields. This is why we all need to be guided into areas in which our talents can be maximized to the fullest. This keeps the world turning evenly and proficiently.

Second, ability says, "Use me or lose me."

Third, most of us use only a portion of the abilities the Creator has given us. We possess potentials we never realize and go through life allowing them to be dormant. Discover yourself. Cultivate your faculties.

Men are often capable of greater things than they perform.

—HORACE WALPOLE

...if any man minister, let him do it as of the ability which God giveth....

—I PETER 4:11

The Plain Truth

On every topic—whether religion, politics, education, finance, security, health—we need the plain, unvarnished truth, the whole truth and nothing but the truth. To be fed pleasant falsehoods is cruelly and monstrously injurious. Moreover, it denies us our basic freedoms—freedom of choice and freedom of action, based on facts.

Half-truth is not sufficient; we can be victimized by the wrong half, and that's a whole lie. Another thing, truth should not be stretched; it's not like a rubber band made to fit the circumstances. We must handle it in its true form. So when you ask for truth, be sure you want it and stay for the answer. If you don't, then you have been false to yourself.

If you tell the truth, you don't have to remember anything.

—MARK TWAIN

Buy the truth, and sell it not....

—PROVERBS 23:23

Be Grateful

We can feed a hungry dog and he won't bite us. Too bad that some people are not that good. Ingratitude is a despicable trait, one of the worst. But gratitude is truly a sign of a noble character.

In addition to saying, "Thank you," we should go further and express our gratitude in deeds, like giving in return. We can and should live the praises due our benefactors. Let's do more than say grace; let's be grateful. And in being grateful, we shall find one source of happiness simply because it doesn't take so much to make us happy if we're truly thankful for what we have.

Gratitude is the fairest blossom which springs from the soul.

—HENRY WARD BEECHER

Be ye thankful.

—COLOSSIANS 3:15

Standing on Understanding

Where understanding is wanting, it's like a blind man feeling his way. Knowledge saves a person from many a fall. For us to stand, we need a support under us: understanding.

Hindsight is better than foresight, but life can't be lived backwards. So the solution is, *Grab some understanding from the past,and shape it into a program for present living.* Understand self; that's the greatest knowledge. Understand people, their backgrounds, views and emotions. Understand the issues of life; by discerning them, we demonstrate a wisdom not found in books. As a first priority, understand the sovereignty of God, for in spite of all our understanding we are still incapable of going it alone.

O divine Master,
grant that I may not so much
Seek...to be understood as to understand.
                              —St. Francis of Assisi

...and with all thy getting get understanding.
                              —Proverbs 4:7

Quality Counts

"A quality person." That's what we have said of different ones. An illustrious compliment. For the greatest measurement of anything or any person is quality. It is not how long you live but how you live that means the most. It is within the power of every person to develop a quality life, but no person can stretch that quantity very far.

In effecting a finer quality, there must be the development of these nobler traits: warm heart, cool head, discerning mind, compassionate eyes, sensitive ears, straight tongue, helpful hands, perseverance, and a sincere commitment to righteousness, truthfulness and fairness. Since such is within the reach of all, let's be superior in quality and let the quantity of days take care of itself.

It is quality rather than quantity that counts.
—SENECA
(8 B.C.-A.D. 65)

Among them that are born of women there hath not risen a greater than John the Baptist: notwithstanding, he that is least in the kingdom of heaven is greater than he.
—MATTHEW 11:11

Beatitudes for Today

 Blessed is he who sees his problems on his knees.
Blessed is he who has an open mind.
Blessed is he who does not "strain at a gnat and swallow a camel."
Blessed is he who does not lose his child's heart.
Blessed is he who maintains his self-respect.
Blessed is he who chooses well the company he keeps.
Blessed is he who does not blow hot and cold with the same breath.
Blessed is he who tries a little harder when others say, "It can't be done."

Blessed is he who has found his work.
—THOMAS CARLYLE

Blessed is the man unto whom the Lord imputeth not iniquity, and in whose spirit there is no guile.
—PSALM 32:2

The Fruit Tells

Behavior is the fruit of the tree which unmistakably tells us the kind of tree that produced it. But there are exceptions, just as one defective apple on a tree does not indict the tree. Occasionally there is an abnormality. So it is with man. A mistake may not picture his true self. However, constant behavior is truly a mirror; it reflects what a person is. I say *constant behavior* because everyone occasionally acts either worse or better than himself.

Beautiful words not backed by meaningful deeds mean nothing. An ounce of *do* is worth a pound of *talk*. People may doubt what you say but not what you do.

Personal behavior is the backbone of our society. Our nation was given to us by the behavior of our founding fathers. Let's hope that it's not destroyed by the behavior of their floundering children.

What you are speaks so loudly that men cannot hear what you say.
—RALPH WALDO EMERSON

And David behaved himself wisely in all his ways; and the Lord was with him.
—I SAMUEL 18:14

Only the Best

P lan for the best. Work for the best. Expect the best. Unambitious average is not good enough. To get the best, each must be his best and do things in the best way. One way is not as good as another. It is as Emerson has stated, "There is always a best way of doing everything, if it be to boil an egg." There are at least two handles to almost every task, and wisdom is needed to know which one to use.

After each of us has become his best, maybe he is still not a masterpiece but he is a full-piece. On second thought, maybe there is no uniform best, only degrees, and he who goes to the *nth* degree has reached the best. That is the last best hope for man.

Give the world the best you have and the best will come back to you.

—MADELEINE BRIDGES

Whatsoever thy hand findeth to do, do it with thy might....

—ECCLESIASTES 9:10

Too Much Crowing

The person who has a right to boast doesn't have to; his deeds praise him. Boasting is one thing, but performing is something else. It's the show-down, not the show-off, that counts. Little bantams are loud at crowing but are not so spectacular when the cockfight starts. And so it is with people; big heads topple easily.

Self-brag is self-backlash. Boasting is mouthing, the ill-advised pompous rhetoric that harms the mouther. But the boaster is unaware that it cuts him down rather than builds him up. He doesn't know that as his head gets too big for his hat, his shoes get too easy to fill. It seems, however, that some are determined to boast even if it's of their own ignorance.

The remedy is found in humility.

The empty vessel makes the greatest sound.
—WILLIAM SHAKESPEARE

Let another man praise thee, and not thine own mouth; a stranger, and not thine own lips.
—PROVERBS 27:2

A Worthy Woman

Woman was made from man's side, and there she belongs. It was Aristophanes (who lived 450-385 B.C.) who said of women, "Can't live with them, or without them." But he was only half right: can't live without them, true; can't live with them, false, for millions do every day. And man is made stronger by the worthy helpmeet at his side. She was made for the role.

She certainly appeals to our finer nature and nobler instincts. Her refinement, charm, empathy, understanding, tenderness, cooperation and love cast a spell over us. And we like it. What wits she has! Obviously she is smart enough to command by obeying and to lead by following. James Russell Lowell paid her this tribute: "Earth's noblest thing, a Woman perfected."

O woman! lovely woman!
Angels are painted fair, to look like you.
— THOMAS OTWAY

...her price is far above rubies.
— PROVERBS 31:10

True Grit

Bravery is not a state devoid of all fear; rather, it is a condition of heart so noble and resolute that it forges ahead in spite of the danger it faces. Maybe the person trembles in his boots, but he doesn't turn heels and run. His ears are tuned to the trumpet's sounds of "Stand" or "Advance," not "Run" or "Surrender."

In deference to this heroic quality, the world usually steps aside for the person brave enough to meet his troubles head-on though he is scared.

History worth reading was written by men and women of grit and backbone. And the future? It too belongs to the brave.

Bravery is the capacity to perform properly even when scared half to death.

—OMAR BRADLEY

Now Naaman, captain of the host of the king of Syria, was a great man with his master, and honorable...he was also a mighty man in valor....

—II KINGS 5:1

When Neutrality Is Wrong

T here is nothing so necessary as being on the right side of the age-old struggle between good and evil. If you are for good, then be for it enough that it compels you to be against its opposite. It was the famous and historic David's love for truth that caused him to say, "I hate every false way." Detest evil. Loathe it. Despise it. As Theodore Roosevelt said, "It is a wicked thing to be neutral between right and wrong."

Widespread abhorrence of evil can go far in cleaning up our land. It can make the world safe for rearing children, wholesome for young people, a joy for couples, and a benediction for the elderly. Its benefits are so priceless.

If more people felt this way, evil would not be having such a field day. Nowadays when evil is popularized and goodness is scorned as a pastime, truly it is past time for us to do something about it.

To enjoy the things we ought and to hate the things we ought has the greatest bearing on the excellence of character.

—ARISTOTLE
(402-317 B.C.)

...Who is on the Lord's side? let him come unto me....

—EXODUS 32:26

Dear Mom

One of the tenderest chords that vibrates in the human heart is the one that is touched by the thought of Mother. Not just because she is a biological necessity of the race. There are other reasons: her tender care in sickness and in health, her dedicated protection day and night, her deepest concern that knows neither clock nor calendar, her unwavering confidence in her child though the child blunders. In her eyes, every son is a king and every daughter a queen.

No sacrifice is too great for a mother to make, and her self-denials are legend. Her rocking chair is the world's most effective schoolroom. Only one other earthly blessing is comparable to having a good mother: a good father. Blessed is the child who has both.

The greatest battle that ever was fought—
Shall I tell you where and when?
On the maps of the world you will find it not:
It was fought by the mothers of men.
—JOAQUIN MILLER

Now there stood by the cross of Jesus his mother....
—JOHN 19:25

A's for Living

Here are the two A's of human development: First, *abound* in everything helpful; second, *abstain* from everything hurtful. If it's bad, keep your foot on the brakes; if it's good, keep your foot off. Happy days never come to those who possess goodness in small or diluted amounts, for joys come only to those who already have it in abundance and absoluteness.

Only a little goodness and a little happiness is no fulfilling program for man. Don't be satisfied with a taste when you can have a full helping. Let's go after the bigger portions; and as we do, we will outgrow the dwarfs who are willing to settle for the crumbs of life.

We have just enough religion to make us hate, but not enough to make us love one another.
—JONATHAN SWIFT

Therefore, as you abound in everything, in faith, and utterance, and knowledge, and in all diligence, and in your love to us, see that ye abound in this grace also [the grace of giving*].
—II CORINTHIANS 8:7

---

*Author's note in brackets.

Intelligent Buying

One way to increase our assets is to watch our spending as carefully as our earnings. The urge to spend does not justify spending. By all means we should never allow ourselves to become addicted to spending. That kind of high can later bring us down low. The only reason for buying anything is to satisfy a want. If it doesn't fill that need, it is worthless.

There are four questions to ask in buying: Do I need it or just think I do? Would something less expensive do as well? Would something else bring greater joy? Is the price right? After answering, a person is intelligently prepared to buy or to decline.

Perhaps the most difficult art in this world for the average person to learn—is the art of intelligent buying.

—A. B. Zu Tavern

She considereth a field, and buyeth it....
—Proverbs 31:16

Measured by Achievement

T his is the long and short of it: Life is measured not by days but by accomplishments, not by how long we have lived but by how much we have done.

There will always be a place for the person who can get the job done. When the rains come (and come they will), there is more refuge in a one-room cabin than in a dream castle.

Every achievement, however, has a price tag and the achiever pays it. Sometimes the price is high, but look at the value received. The achiever is allowed to write his own paycheck. The medals rightly go to him, and they should because he has earned them.

The world is blessed most by men who do things, and not by those who merely talk about them.
—JAMES OLIVER

So built we the wall; and all the wall was joined together unto the half thereof: for the people had a mind to work.
—NEHEMIAH 4:6

Cemetery of Dreams

Dream castles are built by thoughts, but real castles are built by actions. Great thoughts can lead to great achievements; but unless they are acted on, they die and become corpses in the cemetery of Dead Dreams. There the engravings on the headstones are very revealing: "Fear," "Low Priority," "Procrastination," "No Motivation," "Too Demanding," "Too Laborious," and "Much Ado About Other Matters."

Unquestionably we shape our destiny—not by mere thoughts, but by carrying out our thoughts. Action! He who knows and doesn't act is no better off than he who doesn't know.

The greatest achievement was at first and for a time a dream. The oak sleeps in the acorn; the bird waits in the egg.

—JAMES ALLEN

But wilt thou know, O vain man, that faith without works is dead?

—JAMES 2:20

I Shall Be as Gold

I t is easy to discuss the benefits of adversity when we are comfortable, yet the benefits are no less real when misfortune prevails. Then the benefits are just more difficult to accept. So when hardship comes, let's set it to verse and sing away the blues. The difficulty can have hidden compensations.

One benefit of adversity is the effective teaching we receive. Adversity is a school all its own. The tuition is high, but the lessons are telling.

Another compensation of misfortune is that it helps us to become acquainted with ourselves. It brings out our character and values. Opposition spurs some to use religion and others to lose it. Truly the fires of adversity try people and separate the gold from the dross.

Sweet are the uses of adversity.
—WILLIAM SHAKESPEARE

...but he knoweth the way that I take: when he hath tried me, I shall come forth as gold.
—JOB 23:10

Silver Heads

Daily living is as simple as this: Get old or die young. The setting of each sun ends a day, but it can give a clearer view of tomorrow's sunrise. When this happens ten thousand times, think of the growing clarity that can accompany us on our journey. As we ponder the rising and setting of the sun day after day, we develop an inner clarity of vision that physical eyes do not have.

If old age is hopeless, youth has no future. But getting older is not hopeless. While the days are fewer, the rewards can be increased. Youth cannot have the fulness and depth that experience supplies. Rarely do great men of history distinguish themselves before middle age. It is when they are over the hill, so to speak, that they can see better.

It is hard to put old heads on young shoulders.
—AMERICAN PROVERB

With the ancient is wisdom; and in length of days understanding.
—JOB 12:12

Bond of Fellowship

How good and how pleasant it is for people to agree. Consensus puts them on common ground, takes tension out of conversation, and forges a bond of fellowship.

There can be broad agreement when we accept standards and adhere to them: in weights, sixteen ounces as a pound; in measures, twelve inches as a foot; in games, the rules that govern them; in government, the constitution; and in religion, the Bible. Agreement is impossible when each is a law unto himself. In fixed laws and established standards there must be adherence, no deviation from it; and yet, where opinions are concerned, we must grant latitude and have the tolerance to accept differences. With opinions, there can be a kind of agreement in disagreement—an agreement that each is permitted to have his own "think" provided he does not try to force it on another.

The sword within the scabbard keep,
And let mankind agree.

—JOHN DRYDEN

Can two walk together, except they be agreed?

—AMOS 3:3

Lofty Aims

One of the most vital qualities in life is a lofty aim. Aim high or you may wound yourself in the foot. Life's successes are not accidents; they are the marks of aiming—aiming accompanied by trigger-pulling. When we aim, though we miss our target, we will shoot closer to our goal than if we had never tried.

A sure failure is someone who doesn't know where he's going, doesn't know where he is when he gets there and doesn't know where he's been when he returns. An aimless drifter makes nothing happen.

So let us see a star and reach for it.

Not failure, but low aim, is crime.
—JAMES RUSSELL LOWELL

Also I heard the voice of the Lord, saying, Whom shall I send, and who will go for us? Then said I, Here am I; send me.
—ISAIAH 6:8

The Poison of Anxiety

We should have a concern for the things that happen to us; however, we should not permit this interest to develop into nerve-wracking anxiety and weakening strength. Anxiety is quite proficient in seeing what doesn't exist and fretting over what may never happen. More than this, its most gloomy accomplishment is the depression of days and the shortening of life.

Indeed, anxiety is a common poison in our land; it gets into the mind, affects the nerves and frustrates the life. The best antidote is to pull out a dollar—not to spend it, but to read it—and subscribe to its ever relevant and hopeful slogan: "In God we trust." God may or may not remove our burden, but He will give us strength to bear a considerable part of it and allow us to cast the heavier part on Him.

It has been well said that our anxiety does not empty tomorrow of its sorrows, but only empties today of its strength.

—CHARLES SPURGEON

Thou holdest mine eyes waking: I am so troubled that I cannot speak.

—PSALM 77:4

You

You are the key to your future success and stability, happiness and honor. You can take hold of the hand of God and lean on others; but if you advance, you will have to do the walking yourself. You are self-made or self-unmade. Of course circumstances and others enter in, but the real making or breaking is due to you. Your past, whatever it was, you made it. Your present, whatever it is, you are making it. And your future, whatever it will be, you will make it. With God's help. According to an infallible law of God and nature, "Whatsoever a man sows, that shall he reap." You: *individuality.* What you sow: *responsibility.* Now it is up to you to apply the law to the making of a great and beautiful YOU!

You cannot push anyone up a ladder
Unless he be willing to climb himself.
—ANDREW CARNEGIE

For it is God which worketh in you both to will and to do of his good pleasure.
—PHILIPPIANS 2:13

Oil for Troubled Waters

E ach should be big enough and gracious enough to allay misgivings and soothe ruffled feelings. Ordinarily, this can be done by the recognition of another's rights, or tolerance of his faults, or the explanation of a misunderstanding, or an apology for our own blunders, or if principles are not involved a willingness to do a little bending.

Wounds don't need salt; they need a healing ointment. Since like begets like, a gesture of goodwill makes for happier relations. Indeed, appeasement produces goodwill just as an acorn produces an oak tree. Plant it and see the fruit. Take the initiative. Being the first to act is a sign of bigness. If nothing better, at least there is a good chance to achieve agreement in disagreement.

Peace, peace is what I seek, and public calm;
Endless extinction of unhappy hates.
—MATTHEW ARNOLD

A wrathful man stirreth up strife: but he that is slow to anger appeaseth strife.
—PROVERBS 15:18

Approve the Excellent

L et us wholeheartedly and vigorously approve the things that are true, just and excellent. Right needs us on its side, and for our own sake we need to be there. Indeed, we have an index to one's character and faith by observing the things he's for and against. And truly, one cannot be for something without being against something else. Right and wrong are not compatible. Consequently there can be no divided allegiance to them.

Life constantly calls upon all of us to make the decisions of approving and disapproving. Perhaps this note of warning is appropriate: While we condemn evil, may we never become so obsessed with opposing the wrong that we cannot see and applaud the right. May the spirit in this famous quotation never describe us:

All books he reads, and all he reads assails.
—ALEXANDER POPE

...that ye may approve things that are excellent....
—PHILIPPIANS 1:10

Never Argue With a Fool

A rgument is certainly a worthy and noble endeavor (or if you prefer, call it debate or discussion of convictions) but not with everybody under all circumstances and on all occasions. Of course there is never a proper place or time to try to reason with a fool.

Just to say a thing is so does not prove it, and to say it's not so doesn't disprove it. Authority and logic should be employed, and so should good manners. Be careful how you win; you could lose a friend. Just to get the best of the argument is no victory. What counts is proving our point and winning the person to it. Now that unites in mind and spirit and forms a full togetherness.

Don't fool with a fool.

—YIDDISH PROVERB

If a wise man contendeth with a foolish man, whether he rage or laugh, there is no rest.

—PROVERBS 29:9

Wagging Tongues

We live in a world of gossip, but we don't have to indulge in it. The wagging tongue is especially practiced in little towns because everybody knows everybody. Gossip loses much of its appeal when it involves strangers.

It must be an enjoyable pastime or there would not be so many tongues that wag and ears that listen. The fact that so many people do it, however, does not make it right. The mud thrown at others has never cleansed the thrower nor those in the cheer section of the grandstand. Haven't we lived long enough to know that nearly all rumors are false, at least to some extent, enough to change the overall meaning? Indeed, it's better to preach the gospel than to preach the gossip. This will give us a true thrill instead of a perverted one.

Gossip is mischievous, light and easy to raise, but grievous to bear and hard to get rid of.
—HESIOD
(700 B.C.)

Thou shalt not go up and down as a talebearer among thy people....
—LEVITICUS 19:16

Anthill or Mountain

One trait that separates man from the beast is man's longing for something superior, nobler and holier than he has.

How necessary is aspiration! Truly there are no successes where there are no aspirations. He who has no desire to get off the ground assigns himself to the lean fate of a dusty existence.

But aspiration alone is not enough. It takes the combination of aspiration and perspiration to make us winners. They will take us to the top, and the top should be the lofty aim of all. There is no point in standing on an anthill when we can stand on a mountain peak.

Our aspirations are our possibilities.
—ROBERT BROWNING

But the mountain shall be thine....
—JOSHUA 17:18

Thorns in the Flesh

H andicaps can be handled. In many instances what were thought to be liabilities can be turned into assets. The minus (-) is made a plus (+) by striking a line through it. A handicap can cause a person to put forth more effort than usual, and thus his weak point becomes his strong point.

The Apostle Paul had a "thorn in his flesh," probably a physical infirmity; and while God did not answer Paul's prayer to remove it, God did give him grace to bear it. Paul's disadvantage turned out to be advantageous because his strength was made perfect in weakness.

*When thou has thanked thy God for
    every blessing sent,
What time will then remain for
    murmurs or lament?*

—AGNES L. PRATT

...there was given to me a thorn in the flesh, the messenger of Satan to buffet me, lest I should be exalted above measure.

—II CORINTHIANS 12:7

Be Real

The most important thing is to *be,* not to be where you are but simply *to be.* A life needs more than a label; it needs contents. A fine location or position is of little value unless accompanied by a fine person. Just *be* the person that makes it easy to be yourself. Never imitate. Trying to imitate somebody else puts a person on a stressful merry-go-round with no fulfillment. Being yourself, however, does not preclude improvement; for no matter what improvement you make, you're still you. So get busy on yourself.

The best public relations is to *be* , not to *seem.* Counterfeits don't sell. There is no market for phonies.

Be yourself, and the person you hope to be.
—Robert Louis Stevenson

But the wisdom that is from above is...without hypocrisy.
—James 3:17

Sheepskins and Greener Pastures

Graduation! Graduated to what? May it be the going on to:

G —allantry in life's struggles.
R —eadiness unto every good work.
A —cceptance of responsibilities.
D —etermination to succeed.
U —nfeignedness of conduct.
A —lertness to opportunities.
T —argets you have set.
I —mprovement day by day.
O —neness of mind.
N —utriments for the soul.

All that stands between the graduate and the top is the ladder—no elevator.

—ANONYMOUS

Give instruction to a wise man, and he will be yet wiser: teach a just man, and he will increase in learning.

—PROVERBS 9:9

Everyday Valor

The band plays. Flags wave. Excitement is in the air. Warriors are home from the battlefields, and valor is honored. But this is only one kind of bravery.

Heroics are also seen in the everyday affairs of life: In the daily grind of making a living as a common hero keeps on and on. In the household as a person cooks, washes dishes, scrubs floors, diapers babies and does a hundred other things. In human relationships as an offender apologizes. In industry as a worker points out the infractions of right. In a crowd as the person of conviction speaks up. In the pulpit as the preacher refuses to compromise with evil. In the sickroom as a patient suffers pain of body and agony of uncertain days. In the cemetery as loved ones wipe away tears and walk away from the hallowed mound to tie back the broken threads of life.

What is valor? It's not in never being afraid, but in the continuance of the struggle.

*Cowards may die many times before their
    deaths;
The valiant never taste of death but once.*
                    —WILLIAM SHAKESPEARE

...thou mighty man of valor.
                    —JUDGES 6:12

What Is Success?

Each person has his own idea of success, and that idea may change a few times between youth and old age.

Here is mine: Success is strength, enough to stand on our own feet and a little extra to give a lift to a weaker person. Success is acceptance, accepting the hand that is dealt us and nobly playing it to the fullest. Success is effort, perspiration mixed with inspiration. Success is continuance, pushing forward, no holding to yesterday and no fear of tomorrow. Success is happiness, being happy and making others happy. Success is respect, having respect for yourself and gaining the respect of honorable people. Success is righteousness, "to do justly and to love mercy." And finally, success is religion, "to walk humbly with thy God."

There is more to success than sitting on top of the world with your feet hanging off. What about leaving footprints?

—ANONYMOUS

Ponder the path of thy feet, and let all thy ways be established.

—PROVERBS 4:26

Enough Is Enough

The moderate are smart, practical and extremely courageous.

In some matters we need to go all out; but in others we need moderation, such as in our work, our play, a handshake, a visit, a drink of water, a good meal and government. Enough is enough. There can be too much of a good thing. And when we give ourselves too much to one thing, the chances are we give ourselves too little to something else.

Simply put, moderation is just plain old common sense. Extremes face a sure defeat. Even when good goes to extremes, it becomes intolerable. Thus let us live intelligently and moderately.

I will not be a slave to myself, for it is a perpetual, a shameful, and the most heavy of all servitudes.

—SENECA
(8 B.C.-A.D. 65)

And besides this, giving all diligence, add to your faith...temperance....

—II PETER 1:5,6

More Than Rings

M arriage is more than a gown, tuxedo, rings, flowers and presents. For it to be the best, it should be a relationship of two in one. And to be the very best, it should be a relationship of three in one: man, woman and God. It should consist of full devotion, sterling faithfulness, glad helpfulness, shared joys, mutually borne sorrows, united security, and holy procreation of the human race.

With such a closeness and blending, its satisfactions increase—not decrease—with the passing of the years. Marriage is not a failure when it comes to some high hills to climb and some swollen streams to cross. With locked, supportive arms, the journey is easier. No wonder it is held in such high esteem.

The sanctity of marriage and the family relation make the cornerstone of our American society and civilization.

—JAMES A. GARFIELD

Marriage is honorable in all, and the bed undefiled....

—HEBREWS 13:4

Pocket Sermons

M oney is not evil. It's the love of money that is the root of evil, but the lack of money is also the root of much crime. Money itself is amoral—neither good nor bad. It's the attitude toward it and the use that is made of it that determines both. The Bible states that "money is a defense," a defense against hunger, nakedness, street living, bill collectors, public welfare, neglect in illness, and a pauper's grave.

However, money is not worthy of trust, but a dollar bill does say where the trust ought to be: "In God We Trust." A good sermon to carry in your pocket. Trust the God who gives the money rather than trust the money itself. Seen in this light, money has many benefits. Learn its value. Don't pay too high a price for it nor sell it too cheap. Money isn't everything, but it's way ahead of bankruptcy.

How pleasant it is to have money!
—ARTHUR HUGH CLOUGH

And Abram was very rich in cattle, in silver, and in gold.
—GENESIS 13:2

The Old Morality

T he greatest moral code ever given is the Ten Commandments, Exodus 20:1-17. They are directions for running our society. If we break them, we break ourselves, lower our society and weaken our nation. Morality gives a people freedom that mere laws do not provide. It allows people to sleep without fear, leave home without worry, walk the streets without danger, and carry on business and exchange without apprehension.

Opinions change, manners switch and standards modify, but it still remains that any rule or practice that hurts somebody else or even tempts somebody else is morally wrong. The Old Morality worked and is still needed to protect us.

Education without morality breeds only clever criminals.

—THOMAS JEFFERSON

Receive us; we have wronged no man, we have corrupted no man, we have defrauded no man.

—II CORINTHIANS 7:2

Disguised Blessings

T he all-wise Creator thought it productive of good for man's fortune to be interspersed with misfortune. He knew that what is called misfortune can actually be fortune, blessings in disguise. It can subdue us, prompt self-inspection, open our eyes to what we had not seen before, generate thankfulness, reshuffle priorities, divert efforts, renew determination, and stimulate sympathy for the person who is down. These are possible compensations.

The flower that has been crushed has a sweeter aroma than the protected one. We must live through the bleakness of winter to really appreciate the invigoration of spring.

Our toil is sweet with thankfulness,
*   Our burden is our boon;*
The curse of earth's gray morning is
*   The blessings of its noon.*
                    —JOHN GREENLEAF WHITTIER

But as for you, ye thought evil against me; but God meant it unto good....
                    —GENESIS 50:20

Spurs Do Not a Cowboy Make

N either do boots, nor a cowboy hat.

Outward appearances can be very misleading, for true value is not in the box but in the contents. A silver collar does not make a cat a mouser, nor clothes a lady, nor suit a man. A monkey is still a monkey though he is clad in fine clothes. Things are not always what they seem.

While appearances don't make the person, they definitely give insights and make impressions. This being true, it is wise for us to put our best foot forward. This can be done sincerely, free of guise and semblance, by just being our real self.

O what a goodly outside falsehood hath.
—WILLIAM SHAKESPEARE

Judge not according to the appearance....
—JOHN 7:24

When a Slice Would Do

Sometimes what we think are needs are only wishes, and this can be frustrating. Contentment has a better chance of being achieved by those whose needs are few and simple than by those who think they need so much. We may become discontent trying to get a loaf when a slice would have sufficed and by trying to get a house with twenty rooms when actually we can occupy only one at a time.

The only way to understand a real need is to experience it. We can't know the pain of thirst while sipping at a cool, bubbly spring; but when the need becomes critical, it sharpens our wits, opens our eyes, unstops our ears and puts a trot in our steps. Needs spur us to greater accomplishments.

He that is thy friend indeed,
He will help thee in thy need.
—RICHARD BARNFIELD

...let him labor, working with his hands the thing which is good, that he may have to give to him that needeth.
—EPHESIANS 4:28

When Negative Is Positive

T he positive attitude is dynamic and motivating; but let us be aware that every positive has a negative, that one can't be for sobriety without being against drunkenness, or for honesty without being against fraud, or for clean speech without being against vulgarity. This goes with the commitment. So the person who isn't against anything isn't really for anything though he says he is.

Hence, the negative should be given its proper due. God did when He put eight of the Ten Commandments in negative form. The positive can be oversold and the negative underrated. Be neither a blind positive nor a pessimistic negative. Rather, think every matter through and come up with a realistic answer.

If you have a test for cancer, how wonderful if the report is negative instead of positive.
—ANONYMOUS

Thou shalt have no other gods before me [negative*].
—EXODUS 20:3

---

*Author's note in brackets.

Associates Make a Difference

T he most satisfying joys are found in associations. So are the most painful sorrows, the most strength and the most weakness, the most victories and the most defeats. Therefore, let us be wary and discerning in selecting them. Some associates encourage and lift us up the hill with a word of wisdom and a hand that beckons. Others tumble from the heights so fast that it creates a draft that sucks us down with them.

Definitely there is more to associations than the rubbing of elbows. Some of them may rub off on us. No doubt this is why George Washington once said, "It is better to be alone than in bad company." And when we are alone, let's hope we are in good company.

Think not lightly of evil, "It will not come to me." A waterpot is filled by the fall of waterdrops; a fool is filled with evil, amassing it bit by bit.

—SUTTAPITAKA

Make no friendship with an angry man; and with a furious man thou shalt not go; lest thou learn his ways, and get a snare to thy soul.

—PROVERBS 22:24,25

Blessed by Death

Death is grossly and painfully misunderstood. It was appointed to be a blessing, not a curse. Suppose there were no deaths—the old grow older, and the sick become sicker, and there is no relief. Vegetation multiplies, and none of it ever dies. Animals continually reproduce, and none ever expires. Humans enter the world in pyramiding numbers, and none ever departs. This would overcrowd the earth and make life unbearable. Understandably we have to have death to have life.

Furthermore, death is needed to transport us from this world to the one beyond. It is a necessary, sorrowful breaker of earthly ties, but joyfully it was only meant to be temporary!

There is no Death! What seems so is transition.
—HENRY WADSWORTH LONGFELLOW

So when this...mortal shall have put on immortality,...Death is swallowed up in victory.
—I CORINTHIANS 15:54

How to Handle Burdens

Individual responsibility demands that each, to the best of his ability, bear his own burden. But many of our burdens are not real burdens, just imaginary ones. Oftentimes the latter outweigh the former. Unnecessary baggage. How useless! It's not the daily load but the tomorrow's overload that kills. Some burdens can be lightened; if they can, rid yourself of the needless load. If they cannot be lifted, pray for more will and a stronger back.

After doing the best we can, the load may still be too heavy to bear alone. Sometimes fate puts some heavy ones on us, yet there is recourse and hope. First, let our friends give us a shoulder. Second, "Cast thy burden upon the Lord." Then there can be relief and repose.

Burdens become light when cheerfully borne.
—Ovid
(43 B.C.-A.D. 18)

For every man shall bear his own burden.
—Galatians 6:5

More Than a Meal Ticket

An occupation involves an essential of life: work. It is very important that people get into a work that best suits their talents and gives the greatest joy. In choosing an occupation, more than money should be considered: usefulness, peace, gratification. Centuries ago, choices made a farmer out of Cain, a shepherd out of Abel, a fisherman out of Peter, and a carpenter out of Jesus.

See in your occupation something more than a meal ticket. See in it that which blesses others. If you are a baker, see more than a loaf. See the large numbers around dinner tables you are serving. This insight makes it a better job.

Nature fits all her children with something to do.
—JAMES RUSSELL LOWELL

And Pharaoh said unto his brethren, What is your occupation? And they said unto Pharaoh, Thy servants are shepherds, both we, and also our fathers.
—GENESIS 47:3

For an Orderly World

Obedience to civil law is conformity to a necessary system, a system so necessary that God ordained it. Laws, rules and regulations must be obeyed for the safety and good of all. If every person were a law unto himself, a chaotic, unregulated condition would ensue, making freedom and security impossible.

Obedience to nature keeps us in harmony with the universe. Likewise, obedience to God keeps us in harmony with Him, which is so inclusive of all proper laws (religious, moral, civil and natural) that it is aptly called "the whole duty of man."

Let thy child's first lesson be obedience, and the second will be what thou wilt.

—BENJAMIN FRANKLIN

Honor all men. Love the brotherhood. Fear God. Honor the king.

—I PETER 2:17

Mercy Twice Blesses

Mercy has a heart. Puts itself in the other fellow's place. Sees another's woes. Has a helping hand. Recognizes that imperfection is a common weakness. Is inclined to hide the faults it sees. Is forgiving. Is aware that many things are not what they seem. Tempers justice with leniency.

Yet, sometimes mercy requires the painful, such as when the cowboy on the range must mercifully shoot his horse because its leg is broken. Wise mercy is open-eyed—not blind—and sees beyond the present favor, for a thoughtless mercy that turns a criminal loose on the streets is cruelty to those along the streets.

The quality of mercy is not strained;
It droppeth as the gentle rain from heaven
Upon the place beneath: it is twice blest;
It blesseth him that gives and him that takes.
—WILLIAM SHAKESPEARE

Blessed are the merciful: for they shall obtain mercy.
—MATTHEW 5:7

Overcoming Worry

Worry forces a change of tenants in the mind: Sweet peace must move out, and nagging anxiety moves in. Concern is proper and helpful but not worry. Worry is useless, never accomplishes anything, just tears down. Worry is draining, more fatiguing than work and more wearing than exertion.

To overcome worry, develop the right relationship with God, with others and with self. Clean the slate with all three. Let the past be buried. Keep the forward look. Do not cry over spilled milk; there's a cow waiting in the next pasture. Overcome worry with faith. Believe in the sovereignty of God, the power of self, and the goodness of others. Some way, somehow, with the help of all three we make it.

It is not work that kills men; it is worry. Worry is rust upon the blade.
—HENRY WARD BEECHER

The troubles of my heart are enlarged: O bring thou me out of my distresses.
—PSALM 25:17

True Observation

T o get along well in the world, we must keep our eyes and ears open. See. Hear. Observe. This broadens the mind. It brings wisdom.

However, true observation is more than seeing, more than hearing; it is mental. True observation studies the experience and draws conclusions from it. When we see oaks as we look at acorns, our observation has reached the blessed point. Such becomes the parcel of our fortune, for what we see has a great effect on what we get. Hence, be more than a blind bystander; be a seeing observer.

The great sources of wisdom are experience and observation, and these are denied to none.
—WILLIAM ELLERY CHANNING

Seeing many things, but thou observest not; opening the ears, but he heareth not.
—ISAIAH 42:20

Contrary Winds

L ife has its obstacles. But they are God's trainers, and in meeting them we develop into stronger characters. Life is piled high with difficulties. The biggest obstacle, however, is little faith and big fear. So really, the greatest problem is ourselves. We have to overcome ourselves.

While there are many contrary winds, think how smooth the sailing is most of the time. Don't waste time over what we can't change. We can't control the wind. Look ahead. Keep going. And when we face a storm, may God give us strength to grip the oar a little tighter.

It is difficulties which show what men are.
                                        —GREEK PROVERB

And he saw them toiling in rowing; for the wind was contrary to them....
                                        —MARK 6:48

A Father

A good father is worth more than a whole staff of schoolteachers. A father's role is the world's highest calling for any man. His training his children is an immortal service. Perhaps not even fathers themselves can understand the full value of this humble work. A father's duties to head the family, provide for them, protect them, guide them and be a pal to them place heavy burdens on him. But a good father rises to the challenges, reaches down into his heart and comes up with the courage to say, "I can."

How can we honor such a father? As a chip off the old block, the best way to dignify him is to reflect his character and ideals, to be the son or daughter that makes him proud.

So nigh is grandeur to our dust,
So near is God to man,
When duty whispers low, "Thou must."
Father replies, "I can."

—RALPH WALDO EMERSON
ADAPTED

Honor thy father and mother; which is the first commandment with promise....

—EPHESIANS 6:2

Safety in Good Advice

A dvice. This is something most of us need and often don't know it; or if we know it, we unfortunately get it from the wrong sources. Certainly we can get too much advice, especially if we have a bad cold.

Those who think they never need advice cannot be helped. Eagerly seek it and fully consider it; but in the last analysis, each must make his own decision because advice comes in two kinds: good and bad. Sort it out and profit from it.

Get your advice soon enough; after a thing is done, it is too late. Calling a doctor after death is no way to stay alive.

To accept good advice is but to increase one's own ability.
—JOHANN WOLFGANG VON GOETHE

Where no counsel is, the people fall: but in the multitude of counselors there is safety.
—PROVERBS 11:14

Borrowing May Lead to Sorrowing

M oney is sometimes hard to borrow but always harder to pay back, especially if there are carrying charges. This means the debtor has a growing problem; he has to grow in earnings and thrift to meet his obligation. Paying off a loan is an obligation! The borrower's word should be held inviolately.

Hence, he who goes a-borrowing often goes a-sorrowing. Borrowing is a path laden with thorns and pitfalls. The best way to be happy is to live within our means. He who borrows less lives with less worry. Thus we should be cautious and circumspect in borrowing. And when we do borrow, let's be sure our memory is as good as the lender's.

Borrowing is the mother of trouble.
—HEBREW PROVERB

…the borrower is servant to the lender.
—PROVERBS 22:7

My Friend Faith

Faith! Oh, what a friend to unify personality and pull together what would otherwise be a fragmented life. Faith is a friend to arrange priorities and head the list with heart convictions. A friend to protect steps from wandering and keep them within a set path. A friend to give heart and keep the weary traveler from despair. A friend to motivate and mobilize for action. A friend to energize labors and keep the worker from exhaustion. A friend to lift up hands in battle and to put them down in peace. All because of what we believe!

It is good to believe in self and even better to believe in God. And as time goes on, what we believe we become.

If we should be a little short on faith, let us pray in the language of the ancients, "Lord, help thou mine unbelief."

A man lives by believing something.
—THOMAS CARLYLE

...Go thy way; and as thou hast believed, so be it done unto thee.
—MATTHEW 8:13

Better to Trust

I t is better to trust and be deceived sometimes than never to trust at all. Granted, we should be discerning, for a horse that kicks, a dog that shows his teeth, and a person that breaks his word are hardly worthy of trust.

Even our trust in ourselves may sometimes prove to be disappointing. So goes the way of human frailty. Still we have to live with self and with others, and this requires trust. Really there is not but one that is one-hundred-percent trustworthy: GOD. However, people—though they are imperfect—can commend themselves to us in such a manner that we place confidence in them. Our world of commerce and human relations turns on that basis.

It is equally an error to trust all men or no men.
—LATIN PROVERB

Trust in the Lord with all thine heart; and lean not unto thine own understanding.
—PROVERBS 3:5

Revenge Costs Too Much

T he person who seeks vengeance keeps his own wounds open and his own blood pressure up. Revenge is too expensive: It costs him who perpetrates it and him who bears it, even though the perpetrator has to pay the bigger price.

It's more profitable for the sufferer to forget the wrong. Lowering ourselves to the level of evil doers is a poor way to get even. Keeping ourselves above them makes more sense, to be so upright and towering that it's easy to overlook them. When they see that we are so cool, it may burn them to a crisp; but (who knows?) in time our attitude may moderate theirs.

Revenge is often like kicking a mule because he kicks you, and what ensues is a kicking contest.
—ANONYMOUS

Dearly beloved, avenge not yourselves, but rather give place to wrath: for it is written, Vengeance is mine; I will repay, saith the Lord.
—ROMANS 12:19

Unspotted Lives

S pots on the skin are very minor in comparison with spots on the soul. Immoral practices, stretched ethics, dishonest dealings, deceitful manipulations, deceptive reports, dereliction of duties, unbridled tongue, transgressions of the right and holy, and omissions of the good and divine are but a few of the many general examples. Such practices defile and spot persons in the eyes of all who come into contact with them, regardless of whether they are people of good or ill repute themselves.

A religion that does not take us beyond ceremonial observances to a pure life won't sell in the marketplace. Who wants religion without restraint, engagement without enlargement, profession without product, or belonging without being? It is vain!

The purest treasure mortal times afford is spotless reputation.

—WILLIAM SHAKESPEARE

Thou art all fair, my love; there is no spot in thee.
—SONG OF SOLOMON 4:7

Born to Try

Man was born to try. We came into the world trying to get here, tried to nurse, tried to crawl, tried to walk, tried to run, tried to survive. Why should we later quit trying? Giving up is contrary to life. What terrible fate we bring on ourselves when we refuse to try; we lose good days that might be better spent.

Above all, try! Do-nothings say, "If we don't try, we can't lose." But doers say, "If we don't try, we can't win." If we lose, let's lose trying, not by default. Then at least we shall have a moral victory. Indeed there can be no greater compliment for the living and no finer epitaph for the dead than *He Tried.*

I have tried so hard to do the right.
—GROVER CLEVELAND

And Noah began to be a husbandman, and he planted a vineyard.
—GENESIS 9:20

The Cost of Vigilance

O h, what price we pay because we fall asleep at the post or drift without looking up! Vigilance costs a price, but the comfortable state of seeing no danger and hearing no alarm costs more.

The Bible enjoins watchfulness in the protection of the faith. Also, our forefathers emphasized watchfulness for the preservation of our nation. Businessmen, knowing the value of staying alert, keep an eye on where they are and where they are going. And physicians, ever cognizant of health's perils, urge patients to have an annual checkup.

It is better to be on our guard than to be wiped out by our adversary while we sleep. We are too vulnerable to be sleepy. Nothing makes more sense than vigilance.

Eternal vigilance is the price of victory.
—THOMAS JEFFERSON

Be sober, be vigilant....
—I PETER 5:8

Stupidity in Concrete

I rrational stubbornness! It adheres to an expressed opinion, purpose or course in spite of reason, argument or persuasion.

So we need to make a distinction between obstinacy and conviction. Firmness in adhering to right—a refusal to compromise truth—is not obstinacy. Rather, it is conviction which should not be decried, for the world needs more backbone but not the kind of backbone that grows into the brain and destroys all reasoning powers. That is stupidity set in concrete.

A heart that is stubborn for no reason except it wants its way shall fare evil at last.

A savage-creating stubborn-pulling fellow,
Uncurbed, unfettered, uncontrolled of speech,
Unperiphrastic, bombastiloquent.

—ARISTOPHANES
(450-385 B.C.)

Presumptuous are they, self-willed....
—II PETER 2:10

Be Strong

Much of our strength is found in the mind. This is why good coaches work on the mind as well as train the body, why they endeavor to get the players mentally conditioned for the contest. If we think we are weak, we are. If we think we are strong, look out opposition; you have a giant to wrestle! And the more we struggle, the stronger we become.

The faith that God shall sustain us conditions the mind for any and all engagements. When the vicissitude comes, more strength is shown than it seems possible for a person to have. Victory after victory builds up confidence and gives a fearless outlook. We know that with God's help we can handle whatever we have to face.

Be strong!
Shun not the struggle—face it; 'tis God's gift.
—MALTBIE DAVENPORT BABCOCK

Be strong, and quit yourselves like men....
—I SAMUEL 4:9

Mistakes Can Be Valuable

If we do anything, we shall make mistakes. But the person who does nothing makes the biggest mistake of all: not trying.

Yet, mistakes can serve useful purposes. First, they let us see our frailty and imperfection, which should protect us against pride. Second, mistakes should make us more tolerant of others; after all, why should the kettle call the pot black? Third, while mistakes signify faults, they still provide opportunities for us to become bigger by correcting our faults. Fourth, mistakes are the most effective teachers. The wise learn from their mistakes and from the mistakes of others. Fools never learn.

The greatest mistake you can make in this life is to be continually fearing you will make one.
—ELBERT HUBBARD

Cease, my son, to hear the instruction that causeth to err from the words of knowledge.
—PROVERBS 19:27

Easier to Ask Than to Answer

Questions come more easily than answers. This being true, it takes a lot more knowledge and time to answer questions than it does to ask them. Hence, slow answers are often the better part of wisdom. It is comparatively easy to give answers that are only echoes of other voices, but depth, reason and originality are required to give wise answers that fit the questions.

If we think we know all the answers, we simply haven't been asked all the questions. Even a child can ask questions that stump old men and aged women. Neither can you give a clear answer to a vague question. Some questions do not deserve an answer; if they are nonsensical, why dignify them by replying? In some cases the answer can be given in one word and in others by no word at all. Silence can be loud!

Soft words don't wear out the tongue.
—DANISH PROVERB

A soft answer turneth away wrath: but grievous words stir up anger.
—PROVERBS 15:1

Is the Bargain a Bargain?

When buying principles, it is easy to be defrauded. Though the price is marked down, not every trade is a good bargain. He who sells himself or the truth, regardless of the price, always gets the worst of the exchange. Our society needs to hear the relevant words of Solomon, "Buy the truth and sell it not." The truth is worth far more than gold.

Buying and selling can be plain old purse-picking, getting yours picked or picking the other fellow's. Neither has promise. The only view that can last is "Live and let live." Remember, (1) looking for something for nothing is a good way to get cheated, and (2) what you don't need is high at any price. Even a bargain costs something.

What you don't need is dear at a cent.

—CATO
(234-149 B.C.)

And Esau said, Behold, I am at the point to die: and what profit shall this birthright do to me? And Jacob said, Swear to me this day; and he sware unto him: and he sold his birthright unto Jacob.

—GENESIS 25:32,33

Shaped by Causes

E verything is the result of cause. All of life is shaped by the inflexible rule of cause and effect. Every person is what he is, good or bad, due to causes. Bluntly, almost everything that happens to us is initiated by our own action; on occasion, others may cause it.

Talk of changing the effects is useless unless accompanied by a change of causes. What follows is going to depend on what went before. To sow different seed is wiser than to complain about the fruit; for as we sow, so shall we reap.

Shallow men believe in luck; strong men in cause and effect.
—RALPH WALDO EMERSON

Say not thou, What is the cause that the former days were better than these? for thou dost not inquire wisely concerning this.
—ECCLESIASTES 7:10

Wishers and Woulders

The breaking of a wishbone does not break a static condition. It may set the mind aright, but what about the hands and feet? Wishers and woulders are not necessarily dashers and doers, yet there is good in wishing provided it is for the right thing and is hard enough to cause the wisher to do something about it.

In all practicality, however, if we did not spend so much time wishing and spent that time pursuing, we would not have to spend so much time wishing. We would have more, and we would appreciate it more because we would know how we got it.

Looking over the past, we can be glad that we did not always get our wish. Now we know that back then we *didn't* know what was best for us.

If a man could have half his wishes, he would double his troubles.

—BENJAMIN FRANKLIN

Then fearing lest we should have fallen upon rocks, they cast four anchors out of the stern, and wished for the day.

—ACTS 27:29

Honor the Flag

T he flag—the red, white and blue. Old Glory. May it always stand for something. May the red stand for courage, white for cleanness and blue for justice. The flag is more than a piece of cloth; it's a symbol of a people, a nation.

May this nation represented by the flag be clean, free of dirty politics in all its connections and transactions. May it be courageous in the defense and preservation of itself against all destructive forces, inside and outside. May it be just in all its dealings with all people—all races, all colors, all creeds, the poor as well as the rich, the downtrodden the same as the uplifted, the underprivileged as well as the privileged. Then in saluting the flag, we shall be respecting the highest and noblest virtues.

This flag, which we honor and under which we serve, is the emblem of our unity, our power, our thought and purpose as a nation.

—WOODROW WILSON

...Render therefore unto Caesar the things which are Caesar's; and unto God the things that are God's.

—MATTHEW 22:21

Heaven's Masterpiece

M an is the handiwork of God: "Male and female
created he them." Thus man's makeup of both
flesh and spirit should not be discredited. He's
heaven's masterpiece, not nature's mistake. Man's
superiority is on the inside. His brains excel over
brawn. His ability to out-think and out-know all
other creatures on earth makes him the steward
of the earth.

In spite of man's superiority ("a little lower
than the angels") we're still in need of knowing
how to live, and our elevation is found in the
course we take. While abilities vary, it still comes
down to this, as Francis Bacon stated, "The lame
man who keeps the right road outstrips the
runner who takes a wrong one."

*The noblest of all studies is the study of what
man is and of what life he should live.*

—PLATO
(428-348 B.C.)

I will praise thee; for I am fearfully and
wonderfully made: marvelous are thy works....

—PSALM 139:14

Books and Values

Solomon said, "Of making many books there is no end." And there shouldn't be if they are useful and helpful. Of course bookworms can overdo reading and bring on a weariness of the flesh, but we shouldn't protect the flesh at the expense of undernourishing the mind.

In buying a book, a person is getting much more than paper and ink; he receives knowledge, wisdom, insight, stimulus, inspiration, and even a whole new way of life.

Indeed books cannot do our thinking, but they can stimulate us to do our own thinking. As the mind is nourished, so it grows.

It is chiefly through books that we enjoy intercourse with superior minds.... In the best books, great men talk to us, give us their most precious thoughts, and pour their souls into ours.
—WILLIAM ELLERY CHANNING

The cloak that I left at Troas with Carpus, when thou comest, bring with thee, and the books, but especially the parchments.
—II TIMOTHY 4:13

That We Offend Not

Good manners demand that we be not offensive, that we guard against hurting the feelings of others. A sensitivity toward people does not permit us to ignore what is fitting, courteous, and considerate in dealing with them.

Insults can come through impoliteness, harshness, inappreciation, inconsideration and slight. And the slight—a failure to be noticed or to be included—can be the most offensive and painful of all. It's so easy in honoring one to slight another. Even at church when announcements are made concerning the ill, and one person is mentioned and another is ignored, it pleases one family and offends another. All in the same process. We need to be thoughtful.

Old friends become bitter enemies on a sudden for toys and small offenses.

—ROBERT BURTON

A brother offended is harder to be won than a strong city....

—PROVERBS 18:19

Neutrality Can Be Cowardice

Neutrality is permissible and sometimes advisable when nothing of real importance is involved but *not* when things that really count are at stake. Not when the battle rages between truth and error. Not when morality is perverted into immorality. Not when the sanctity of the home is under attack. Not when the welfare of the country is threatened. Not when Christianity is in combat with the world.

The very nature of some struggles will not permit neutrality. Just to do nothing puts one on the side of error, wrong and evil.

In the battle of right and wrong, the neutralist is a cowardly duck who doesn't quack.
—ANONYMOUS

He that is not with me is against me; and he that gathereth not with me scattereth abroad.
—MATTHEW 12:30

Showers of Blessings

B lessings—we all have many. Misfortunes—we all have some, which in most instances are due to our own follies. Then in this mixture of helps and hurts, we handicap ourselves further if we see mostly the mishaps instead of the bounties. It destroys morale and casts us into a no-win role. There will always be things we don't have, but their importance will shrink as we count our blessings.

If our vessel is empty, we can still count our blessings, for we still have the vessel. We just need to roll up our sleeves and fill it. "Work to have" is God's ringing message.

As we count our blessings, let's remember to thank the Blesser. As our cup runs over, let's ever acknowledge that God lent a hand and then let's place the runover in trust for the benefit of others.

Let not the blessings we receive daily from God make us not to value or not to praise him because they be common.

—GEORGE ELIOT

And I will make them and the places round about my hill a blessing; and I will cause the shower to come down in his season; there shall be showers of blessing.

—EZEKIEL 34:26

Heart Bonds

S tanding together in a cause is much more supportive and enjoyable than standing alone. It is man's
nature to seek the companionship of people with
like minds, like aims and like efforts. Mutual
likes form heart bonds and make partners. We
call it fellowship. Just eating together, however, is
not fellowship but rather may be a fruit of fellowship, the coming together and eating together because of similar interests. Similar interests—
that's the binding tie.

Certainly fellowship is not the cure of all our
ills, but it does make those ills easier to bear, the
joys more enjoyable to share, and the drooping
spirits easier to rise again. It's more than physical
presence. It's the like beatings of human hearts.

*What men call good fellowship is commonly but
the virtue of pigs in a litter which lie close together to keep each other warm.*
                                    —HENRY DAVID THOREAU

...for what fellowship hath righteousness with
unrighteousness? And what communion hath
light with darkness?
                                    —II CORINTHIANS 6:14

There Is a Time

Correct timing is extremely important in achieving success. Its urgency has given rise to such maxims as "Strike while the iron is hot" and "A stitch in time saves nine." It's the easier way. Hence, there can be Solomonic wisdom in the simple statements, "Now is the time" or "Now isn't the time."

Observe due measure, for right timing is in all things the most important factor.

—HESIOD
(700 B.C.)

To everything there is a season, and a time to every purpose under the heaven: a time to be born, and a time to die; a time to plant, and a time to pluck up that which is planted; a time to kill, and a time to heal; a time to break down, and a time to build up; a time to weep, and a time to laugh; a time to mourn, and a time to dance; a time to cast away stones, and a time to gather stones together; a time to embrace, and a time to refrain from embracing; a time to get, and a time to lose; a time to keep, and a time to cast away; a time to rend, and a time to sew; a time to keep silence, and a time to speak; a time to love, and a time to hate; a time of war, and a time of peace.

—ECCLESIASTES 3:1-8

A Balanced Life

Balance, self-control and poise are constantly needed to meet life's troublesome and vexing experiences. If we lose our balance, down we go.

By all means, keep yourself in balance, in check. Guard against extremes. Anything can be under-done or overdone. Hold your balance and especially the moment something doesn't go your way.

There are many tightropes to walk, and only the person of balance can traverse them. Though at times he may sway a little, he doesn't fall off. He keeps his head and walks his course, weighs the situations and issues and then answers out of calmness and reason.

Moderation in all things.

—TERENCE
(190-159 B.C.)

Hold thou me up, and I shall be safe: and I will have respect unto thy statutes continually.
—PSALM 119:117

Let Tears Flow

Weeping shows emotion. So does laughter, but not everything in the world is a matter of laughter. There are also heartbreaking situations, and when the heart responds by breaking, it is only natural (unless repressed) that the tears flow. The heart pressured with sorrow finds an outlet in weeping. It is then that we feel better—after the cry.

So endowed, man should not quench the heart nor stop its faucet. Simply, the mourning should be a sincere pattern of naturalness. Do not hold back the tears when they should come nor force them when they shouldn't flow. Not chronic blubber, but natural and timely weeping.

She must weep or she will die.
—ALFRED LORD TENNYSON

...weeping may endure for a night, but joy cometh in the morning.
—PSALM 30:5

A Virtuous Life

Virtue firmly ties a person to high standards and gives him peace in times of quiet and stability in times of storm. It chooses the good part and the clean life. It is found in a determination to do what is right. It shows courage to stay put when evil forces would sweep him away.

Virtue does not consist in no temptation but in the resistance of it. Virtue will not be stampeded into conformity; it says *No.* Virtue is found in strength of character, which is never known until one has passed through the biddings. The higher the bid, the more character it takes not to sell out.

There was never yet any truly great man that was not at the same time virtuous.

—BENJAMIN FRANKLIN

...add to your faith virtue....

—II PETER 1:5

The Struggle

Our world is a world of struggles. The earth struggles to make another orbit. The planted seed struggles to germinate and break the soil. The little bird in the nest exerts itself to fly. The baby strives to walk. Since that first step we have faced a thousand challenges, and the struggle goes on and on; and that's all right, for we were made for it. There is nothing to fear though the struggle is strenuous.

We don't mount the mountain peak with one step. It's a long, laborious effort that requires application, planning, pursuit and perseverance. And the effort to go higher and higher develops character and gives satisfaction with every step. So let us climb, striving for more than bread—for our ideals.

The virtue lies in the struggle.
—ALAN ALEXANDER MILNE

...which have borne the burden and heat of the day.
—MATTHEW 20:12

Tales That Wag

B e wary of tales. So often the tale wags the society. What we don't know is that it could have originated in either honest misunderstanding, or in vested interest that made it glow, or in dishonest vengeance coming from the lying lips of an enemy. A tale once told can be shaped according to the teller; twice told, a little different; and a hundred times told, very different.

Hence, before giving a story credence, it's necessary to know how and why it got started, how correct it was originally, and if it's the same now as it was when first told. This emphasizes the need for discernment. We shouldn't believe every tale. Since dead men tell no tales, when tales are going around, we ought to play dead.

Tale-bearers are as bad as the tale-makers.
—RICHARD BRINSLEY SHERIDAN

The words of a talebearer are as wounds....
—PROVERBS 18:8

Refined by Affliction

Affliction has the power to make us sad, but when properly appropriated it can sober us. Affliction can make us search for life's "whys"; and in so doing, we can find in the recesses of the mind a deeper wisdom. Affliction becomes our teacher; it schools us in virtues that we might not otherwise acquire.

Most of life's deeper lessons have to be learned from trouble; otherwise we shall not fully understand them. This lets us see a wisdom that is not visible on the surface. We learn by observing the limping man but not nearly so much as when we walk in his shoes and feel the tack within.

Afflictions clarify the soul.

—FRANCIS QUARLES

Behold, I have refined thee, but not with silver; I have chosen thee in the furnace of affliction.

—ISAIAH 48:10

Life in the Real World

The real me has to live in the real world. No amount of emotionalism and dreamy imagination will change it. After we are carried away in dream clouds, we still have to come back down to earth. That's where we live.

Hence, dreams, imaginations and plans should be regulated by reality. We can't ignore actuality. Neither can we run from it, nor can we bypass it. We have to face things as they are and not as we would like. Fancy says, *Flap your arms and fly,* but reality says, *Build an airplane.* Fancy says, *Take one step to the mountaintop,* but reality says, *Climb, climb, climb.* And that's practical!

Take the world as it is, not as it should be.
—GERMAN PROVERB

…they kindled a fire, and received us everyone, because of the present rain, and because of the cold.
—ACTS 28:2

The Devil's Darling Sin

A person can stand so tall in his own mind that he cannot lower himself enough to rub shoulders with others. Though he has elevated himself, the populace doesn't look up to him, and it will not do him any good to feign a kind of humility in his pride. The proud often wear the garb of superiority, but it's too thin; we can see through it. Really, maybe the self-exalted did stand above others until he started thinking he did. Then how he fell!

Being humble doesn't make a person a fool; Jesus is proof of this. It's our thinking too highly of ourselves that is foolish and self-defeating, for it's at the bottom of nearly all social mistakes. When pride lifts its conceited head, everything goes wrong.

And the Devil did grin, for his darling sin
Is pride that apes humility.
—SAMUEL TAYLOR COLERIDGE

Pride goeth before destruction, and a haughty spirit before a fall.
—PROVERBS 16:18

Strength in Weakness

Weakness is something all of us have at times, the difference being in the times, the areas and the degrees. And no person is ever so weak as when he thinks he's so strong that he's unassailable and unbreakable. This admonition is needed: "Let him that thinketh he standeth take heed, lest he fall." Then because of his caution, Scripture reading and prayer, his strength grows out of his weakness.

Still, there are times when we are all abnormally weak, but this does not make us weaklings. A weak board is not apt to cause the house to collapse, but a weakling—his life has already caved in.

You cannot run away from a weakness; you must sometime fight it out or perish; and if that be so, why not now, and where you stand?
—ROBERT LOUIS STEVENSON

...for when I am weak, then am I strong.
—II CORINTHIANS 12:10

Time Management

The most valuable part of anyone's capital is time—more precious than gold. It is the most expensive commodity we can spend, for the amount is limited and irreplaceable.

Indeed, sound economics demands more than the wise handling of money; it includes the expedient management of time, which means the judicious supervision of self. To do this, the more important things must be given priority; then organize; next, pursue the goal; and last, do not be deterred by distractions—hold them to a minimum. That's applied time. It gets things done. It's more than counting years—it's making years count.

Time is what we want most, but what alas! we use worst.

—William Penn

So teach us to number our days, that we may apply our hearts unto wisdom.

—Psalm 90:12

Moments of Quietness

"Be quiet." This admonition was spoken by our parents to us noisy kids. Our parents' frayed nerves were crying out for some relief. Most of us can relate to their urgent need. For our nerve-racking life style is filled with noise, chatter, uproar, excitement and pressure.

Many families are weakened and tattered by an endless chain of pressing events, bedlam, pandemonium and discord. A few quiet hours at home would be a tonic for the soul and a balm for the nerves. Thus for a stronger character and a happier life, find some quietness and silence every day. This will rest the brain, relax the body and deepen the insight.

I have often said that all the misfortunes of men spring from their not knowing how to live quietly at home.

—BLAISE PASCAL

...in quietness and in confidence shall be your strength....

—ISAIAH 30:15

The Prison of Prejudice

There is nothing stronger and harder to break out of than prejudice. Prejudice is stronger than steel; it makes a prison of one's mind, locks it up, and bars it from considering the truth or falsity, the right or wrong, of a matter. Prejudice is not a case of holding opinions but rather a case of opinions holding the person.

Prejudice wears the garb of reason but is too small to cover the real facts since bias is a view with nothing to support it. When prejudice selects a political candidate, his opponent isn't likely to get much consideration. And when prejudice picks a religion, the Bible is apt to go unexamined.

A great many people think they are thinking when they are merely rearranging their prejudices.

—WILLIAM JAMES

He that hath ears to hear, let him hear.
—MATTHEW 11:15

Judicious Counsel

N o matter how wise and prudent we are, counsel is always advisable. No one can know everything on every topic, which makes counsel a universal need, but it is something that should be sought and considered with care. Injudicious advice is worse than no advice. So when counsel is received, always weigh it. Sleep on it.

If it is good, take it no matter who gives it; but generally speaking, don't give it unless it is asked. In time, the years become a smart counselor to the judicious, for experience teaches more easily than books and people.

To give counsel to a fool is like throwing water on a goose.

—DANISH PROVERB

The way of a fool is right in his own eyes: but he that hearkeneth unto counsel is wise.

—PROVERBS 12:15

Fidelity Distinguishes Us

F idelity—careful observance of duty, conscientious discharge of obligations, unwavering loyalty—is a MUST in the formation of a real man or woman. To him or her, commitments are binding, words are bonds, and oaths are oracles. Such a person can't be bought and never wavers with fortune. In a society wounded and bled by trickery and deceit, he is our second last hope for sanity: The first is God, and the second is God's working through people like him.

Unquestionably, fidelity is the foundation of every great success; without it, there is no rock on which to build. It is basic, so noble that it exalts even the humblest servant. To be famous without it is a recognition undeserved, just a sham. To be recognized for it is a distinctive honor.

Nothing is more noble, nothing more venerable than fidelity.

—CICERO
(106-43 B.C.)

But I trust in the Lord Jesus to send Timotheus shortly unto you, that I also may be of good comfort, when I know your state. For I have no man likeminded, who will naturally care for your state.

—PHILIPPIANS 2:19,20

The Good Life

It is much easier to be good if we have God in our lives. If God is taken out of "good," nothing is left but 0. Clearly one of the ways we serve God is to do good to man.

Mark Twain said, "Be good and you will be lonesome," but I think there are more good people out there than he thought.

Being good pays great dividends; it is good for one's soul, health, self-respect, and also for public relations, fellowship and success. Any religion that does not put goodness into a person and take goodness out of him is a failure.

He who stops being better stops being good.
—OLIVER CROMWELL

Then tidings of these things came unto the ears of the church which was in Jerusalem: and they sent forth Barnabas.... For he was a good man....
—ACTS 11:22-24

Keep on Singing

T he optimist is right more times than the pessimist; but even if he isn't, think how much more fun he has. And when he gets the worst of it, his outlook enables him to make the best of it. The pessimist looks at the cloud and sees a storm, but the optimist looks at it and sees showers of blessings. On the law of averages, the optimist is right, for there are many more gentle rains than storms.

Oh, how we could learn from the teakettle; when it's up to its neck in hot water, it keeps on singing.

In looking at a doughnut the pessimist sees the hole but the optimist sees the whole.

—ANONYMOUS

Commit thy way unto the Lord; trust also in him, he shall bring it to pass.

—PSALM 37:5

Inspiration Plus Perspiration

Inspiration is a heart effect, an enlivenment and animation of the heart. It is born of new thoughts, rekindled thoughts, increased faith, insight to opportunities, awakening of hopes and sometimes of desperation. "The last straw on the camel's back" doesn't always break it; sometimes it's the inspiring urge to make it.

It is advantageous to be lifted into the silvery clouds provided you can come back down to earth where perspiration is an essential part of life. All hands and no heart will not suffice, and neither will all heart and no hands. May we have the combination of the two.

Genius is one percent inspiration and ninety-nine percent perspiration.
—THOMAS A. EDISON

My heart was hot within me; while I was musing the fire burned....
—PSALM 39:3

The Monster Within

Jealousy! The Bible calls it cruel. Shakespeare calls it a monster. I call it self-destructive. Jealousy often destroys what it would like to keep; for instance, a child refused to let a playmate hold the kitten she held. Instead, she clamped down tighter and tighter and actually killed what she wanted. Jealousy may cause a person to hold a love or a connection so tightly that he kills it. A jealousy that does not permit breathing room for the object of love is destructive.

When not contained, jealousy is a self-torment that torments others. It is born of misgiving and nourished by doubt. For it to be overcome, one's thinking must be changed.

The venom clamors of a jealous woman
Poison more deadly than a mad dog's tooth.
—WILLIAM SHAKESPEARE

For jealousy is the rage of a man: therefore he will not spare in the day of vengeance.
—PROVERBS 6:34

Expectant Asking

"Ask and ye shall receive," declared Jesus. Nineteen centuries have not outmoded its efficacy. Indeed, fortune favors him who asks, provided he knows how to do it. Improper asking, however, can be worse than useless, can actually cause the loss of what one already has. Nevertheless, proper asking doesn't cost anything. It's the *not* asking that can be very expensive, resulting in the loss of directions, overpayment of prices, bungling of jobs, loss of the considerations of man and of the blessings of God.

Never be too proud to ask. I didn't say beg; I said *ask*. Have you noticed that the getters are the askers? They're the elected officials, employed workers, and married persons (at least one of them). Ask wisely. Ask expectantly. For the response to a request can be a hand of blessing.

Asking costs nothing.

—AMERICAN PROVERB

Ye have not, because ye ask not.

—JAMES 4:2

Motes and Beams

One thing we need to guard against is intolerance. For all err. We don't have enough perfection to be self-righteous nor enough superexcellence to be inconsiderate of others' faults. When we realize that we are all made of the same clay and any mistake made by another could have been made by any of us under the same circumstances, that should make us tolerant. This plea for leniency is not the encouragement of evil but a sympathetic and understanding attitude toward him who has erred. If the faulty person can stand himself all the while, then surely we can stand him a little while once in awhile. Furthermore, he who will have only perfect associates must resign himself to no associates.

I have learned silence from the talkative, toleration from the intolerant, and kindness from the unkind; yet strange, I am ungrateful to those teachers.

—KAHLIL GIBRAN

And why beholdest thou the mote that is in thy brother's eye, but perceivest not the beam that is in thine own eye?

—MATTHEW 7:3

Blessing of Open-mindedness

Some doors open when we approach, but not all minds are that functional. In all candor, a closed mind has closed the door on knowledge, improvement and opportunity. It won't permit a little self to get any smarter or bigger. To get the most out of life in all fields—financial, political, social and religious—one needs to keep an open mind.

By opening the mind, one gives ventilation to his soul and protects himself from the stench of prejudicial decay. Furthermore, it grants freedom. No person is free whose mind is closed. It is either be the slave of prejudice or the freeman of open-mindedness.

I shall try to correct errors when shown to be errors.

—ABRAHAM LINCOLN

And when they heard of the resurrection of the dead, some mocked: and others said, We will hear thee again of this matter.

—ACTS 17:32

Road of Intentions

I ntention is one thing. Accomplishment is something else. However, every great accomplishment had to begin with an intention. It didn't happen accidentally. But intentions alone blow only dreamy bubbles that quickly burst. Sickly, paralytic intentions only breathe for a while, then die, and are buried in the mind's cemetery of buried intentions.

"The road to hell is paved with good intentions," we're told. So is the road to heaven. The difference is that on the road to heaven, the intentions are carried out.

Hell is full of good intentions or desires.
—ST. BERNARD BERNARD

And we went before to ship, and sailed unto Assos, there intending to take in Paul.
—ACTS 20:13

We Are Brothers

It is very evident that all of us originated from a common ancestry. Here we are flesh of the same flesh, bone of the same bone, and blood of the same blood. This makes us brothers: brothers to all the kings, queens, noblemen and achievers that ever lived; and by virtue of the fact that we're all in the same human family—whether we like it or not—we're also brothers to all the criminals, liars, cheats and failures that have tarnished the race.

This should waken within us the desire to stand together, to help each other, and to improve the race. For we are brothers. We are our brother's keeper. And how necessary it is for him, and how satisfying it is for us!

Brotherhood is not just a Bible word. Out of comradeship can come and will come the happy life for all.

—HEYWOOD BROUN

And Abram said unto Lot, Let there be no strife, I pray thee, between me and thee, and between my herdsmen and thy herdsmen; for we be brethren.

—GENESIS 13:8

Supported by Uprightness

The upright may not be the upper crust. Nor the lower crust. Uprightness depends on what we are on the inside. The heart is the making of the man. It is the good and honest heart that is commended in the Scriptures. And that is what we should keep with all diligence, for out of it comes the deportment that makes us upright or low-down.

To be upright, we cannot lower ourselves to the level of evil, nor bow to the counsel of the ungodly, nor sit in the seat of the scornful. We have to stand up, stand on our own feet, unbowed, unbended. To do this, we must have something on the inside to support us.

A man should be upright, not be kept upright.
—MARCUS AURELIUS ANTONINUS
(A.D. 121-180)

Let integrity and uprightness preserve me.
—PSALM 25:21

Let Arbitration Settle the Difference

In our dealings with each other there is always the possibility of disruptive conduct, chilling offense, and breached relations. It may reach the point where one feels that he has been mistreated or exploited or defrauded. Moreover, the buds of ruffled feelings often blossom into bitter controversy.

Action is needed to right the wrong and to pacify the widening alienation. First, in a spirit of love and reconciliation a personal effort should be made to reach an understanding. If this fails, then the matter should be submitted to arbitration. Let good, wise and uninvolved people decide what prejudice or selfishness or stubbornness cannot solve. And if they fail, be patient; for maybe time will arbitrate what humans cannot handle.

Better an egg in peace than an ox in war.
—AMERICAN PROVERB

Is it so, that there is not a wise man among you? no, not one that shall be able to judge between his brethren?
—I CORINTHIANS 6:5

Unimportant Trifles

Never be disturbed by unimportant trifles. Pass them by for the things that count, for the weighty issues that make a difference. Ordinarily we can tell the size of a person by what absorbs him. Still, little things—as well as big things—can be very crucial and should be tended.

It is the little things of no consequence that should not be given priority. Never make something of nothing. There are enough real facts, problems and issues that need attention. Making mountains out of molehills is not a construction job—just an imagination job. Definitely it is not wise to traffic with senseless trifles. No profit. Just a waste of time.

Dispense with trifles.

—WILLIAM SHAKESPEARE

Neither give heed to fables and endless genealogies, which minister questions, rather than godly edifying which is in faith: so do.

—I TIMOTHY 1:4

What Climbs Mountains

L ow ambition never climbs a high mountain, nor fords a broad river, nor builds a tall skyscraper. It never makes much of a mark in the world. Rather, it sits down and silently and passively watches the world go by, leaving the unaspiring behind, rocking, rocking in their mocking chair, dreaming, dreaming, but never waking up. But the wide-awake accomplishers catch a vision and pursue it with all their might.

Of course, ambition is no substitute for ability, but what is the benefit of ability without it? It's like a car without fuel—the ability is there but nothing to propel it.

We must keep our ambition headed in the right direction. Then on with it. For we are measured by our goals.

I find the great thing in this world is not so much where we stand, as in what direction we are moving.
—OLIVER WENDELL HOLMES, SR.

And they said, Let us rise up and build. So they strengthened their hands for this good work.
—NEHEMIAH 2:18

That Thief

There's no way to make up for lost time. We may procrastinate, but time doesn't. It keeps speeding on schedule—never late. So really, "procrastination is not the thief of time," but rather the thief of responsibility and opportunity. That's what it steals.

When we put off until tomorrow what should be done today, we are doubling tomorrow's problems. Even worse, we are putting accomplishment on death row. That Old Man Procrastination is a sure executioner ready to kill every good idea we have.

Don't tie yourself to the post—postponement. Tomorrow! Tomorrow! is only a mirage! The best way to take care of the future is to take care of the present. Start now!

While we are postponing, life speeds by.

—SENECA
(8 B.C.-A.D. 65)

Go to now, ye that say, Today or tomorrow we will go into such a city, and continue there a year, and buy and sell, and get gain: Whereas ye know not what shall be on the morrow.

—JAMES 4:13,14

Beset by Troubles

Troubles! Troubles! A world of troubles! And it's easy for each of us to think he has more than anybody else. Though they are bothersome, troubles have their compensations: They give an empathy, a mercy and a toughness that could never develop if life's highway were free of bumps.

In handling trouble: (1) Be sure it's real, not the product of an overworked imagination. (2) If it's actual, don't magnify it out of proportion. (3) Make up your mind that you, with God's help, can handle it—never think of defeat. (4) Deliberate—do not jump from the frying pan into the fire. (5) Fully handle it—not halfway, for this would double the trouble. (6) In conclusion, never seek trouble—enough will find you.

I am an old man and have known a great many troubles, but most of them never happened.
—Mark Twain

Yet man is born unto trouble, as the sparks fly upward.

—JOB 5:7

Making Ourselves Useful

If I support my family, I'm a provider.
If I kiss a child's hurt finger, I'm a healer.
If I dry another's tear, I'm a comforter.
If I reach a hand to the fallen, I'm a restorer.
If I give directions to a lost pilgrim, I'm a guide.
If I work for harmony, I'm a peacemaker.
If I right the world's wrongs, I'm a crusader.
If I hearten the despondent, I'm an encourager.
If I aid the needy, I'm a benefactor.
If I keep secrets, I'm a confidant.
If I light a candle in a dark world, I'm an illuminator.
If I live a sermon, I'm an example.
If I'm just a part of this, I'm useful.

We must assist one another, it is the law of nature.

—FRENCH PROVERB

Thou shalt help me...then I will come and help thee.

—II SAMUEL 10:11

Acceptance Makes Life

When there can be a conscientious acceptance, go for it. This saves unnecessary struggles. It makes life easier. It lets you swim downstream.

What needs changing that can be changed, change it; what can't be changed, accept it. Rebelling at unalterables just makes them worse. The first step to progress is to accept the condition where we are. That acceptance of the present can be the basis for something better in the future. Then we are ready to figure out how to cope with it and go from there.

O God, give us serenity to accept what cannot be changed, courage to change what should be changed, and wisdom to distinguish the one from the other.

—REINHOLD NIEBUHR

But now he is dead, wherefore should I fast? can I bring him back again? I shall go to him, but he shall not return to me.

—II SAMUEL 12:23

Escape From Boredom

I f life is boresome to you, think what you may be to others. There is a happier role. Man's challenge is to find interest and to be interesting. Human life is much too short to bore yourself or others.

Here are six ways to save ourselves from being bored: (1) Have some challenge in life; that which is too easy becomes tiresome. (2) Set some worthwhile goals; don't just drift. (3) Work; idlers become listless. (4) Help others; this takes the mind off the boredom of living in a little world no bigger than self; it fills the days with interest; it brings joy and satisfaction. (5) Get fun from associations and activities with others. (6) Keep your mind alive; keep it out of a self-made morgue; read, study, think.

Bore, a person who talks when you wish him to listen.

—AMBROSE BIERCE

Withdraw thy foot from thy neighbor's house; lest he be weary of thee, and so hate thee.

—PROVERBS 25:17

United We Stand

W here unity dwells there is multiplied strength. "A threefold cord is not quickly broken." The unity of several is needed for the survival of each. The lone sheep has less protection than the flock. When we stand together in the spirit of "all for one and one for all," it protects each and all.

Don't mistake union, however, for unity. Union is a physical togetherness though the hearts may be far apart. Two cats tied together and thrown over a clothesline constitute union but not unity. To have unity we must be of the same mind and walk by the same rule. Let that mind be the mind of Christ and that rule the Scriptures. They pull people of diverse backgrounds into a beautiful, strong and effective unity.

United we stand, divided we fall.

—G.P. MORRIS

Behold, how good and pleasant it is for brethren to dwell together in unity.

—PSALM 133:1

Like a Tree

There are powerful sermons to learn from the tree:
(1) It was once a twig—our children are tomorrow's adults. (2) As the twig is bent, so grows the tree—early influences are life-shaping. (3) The older the tree, the harder it is to bend—age inclines us to become set in our ways. (4) It is known by its fruit—no one can argue with a demonstration. (5) Only the tree that bears fruit gets threshed or has rocks thrown at it—destroyers of reputation find no fun in attacking fruitless people. (6) The taller the tree, the harder it falls—when big people fall, the reverberations are deafening. (7) A straight tree can have crooked roots—don't let uncomplimentary ancestors shape your standing. (8) The deeper the roots, the stronger the winds the tree can withstand—depth protects us from stress and strain.

Only God can make a tree.

—JOYCE KILMER

And he shall be like a tree planted by the rivers of water, that bringeth forth his fruit in his season.

—PSALM 1:3

Judgment Shapes Our Destiny

So much depends on judgment, we shape our destiny every time we use it. Better be sure it's good! People complain of their background, training and opportunities, but not their judgment. Yet it may be the real cause of their plight. It may be too unknowledgeable, too shallow, too biased, too hasty, too moved by temporary circumstances, too swayed by the present moment, too open-eyed to the portion and too blind to the whole, and too proud to consult others.

Thoroughness and slowness are marks of superior judgment. On the other hand, snap judgment usually leads to broken hopes. Be thorough. Take time.

Young in limbs, in judgment old.
—WILLIAM SHAKESPEARE

O that they were wise, that they understood this, that they would consider their latter end!
—DEUTERONOMY 32:29

The Brightest Keys

Each of us is the human key to many locks—situations. There are some doors, however, for which we are not the key; never crash them. We were not made for every lock. Be thankful we weren't. For we would be too many jangling keys on an impractical ring.

But God the great Locksmith has fashioned every individual into a key for some locks—locks that should be opened. And as we do, we shall continue to be effective. For only the keys that are used stay bright. Be encouraged. Usually it is the last key on the ring that works. Maybe the world—at least a part of it—is just waiting for us.

The used key is always bright.
—BENJAMIN FRANKLIN

Go, and the Lord be with thee.
—I SAMUEL 17:37

Goodness in Action

Sympathy is a tender feeling of the heart, but kindness is that feeling in motion. It does something; it is goodness in action. It is a friend maker. A friend keeper. Bread for the hungry. Shelter for the homeless. Medication for the sick. Ointment for bruised hearts. Hand for the fallen. Voice of gentleness. Oil for troubled waters. And an effective weapon that can disarm an enemy.

Kindness is one of the clearest ways to express true religion. For a religion that is not kind is only surface-deep and superficial, lacking in the distinctive quality of love and consideration.

A kind heart is a fountain of gladness, making everything in its vicinity freshen into smiles.
—WASHINGTON IRVING

And be ye kind one to another.
—EPHESIANS 4:32

More Than Kin

"**B**lood is thicker than water," we are told. Yes, provided all other things are equal, but sometimes all other things are not equal. The same blood may flow through the veins but not necessarily the same thoughts through the mind. Family members may be alike in looks but different in ways. So much so that they oppose each other and fight among themselves. This difference runs all the way back to Cain and Abel who were akin in flesh but not in spirit.

So the strongest kinship tie is the spirit's cord. Likemindedness and common purposes make brothers and sisters of us all. The best place to find this is in the church, the family of God. There we become part of a new family tree.

A little more than kin, and less than kind.
—WILLIAM SHAKESPEARE

And at the second time Joseph was made known to his brethren; and Joseph's kindred was made known unto Pharaoh.
—ACTS 7:13

Power in a Smile

There is winning power in a smile: Power to relax the smiler. Power to set at ease the observer. Power to produce a magnetism that draws others. Power to warm associations when coldness prevails. Power to cool relations when sparks begin to fly. Power to cultivate optimism and tend us toward looking on the bright side. Power to spread from one face to another. A smile is apt to get a smile in return. As the smiles multiply, we scatter sunshine over the land.

This power is free and available to all. Let us appropriate it. As we do, the world welcomes us.

So, pack up your troubles in your old kit-bag.
And smile, smile, smile.

—GEORGE H. POWELL

A merry heart maketh a cheerful countenance.

—PROVERBS 15:13

Flowers of Appreciation

When appreciation and flowers are due, freely give them—not backhandedly, but directly and sincerely. By applauding, we help two people: him and ourselves. Handing out flowers sweetens the atmosphere.

Whatever is done for us should be appreciated—tell the donors. Whatever is of merit should be applauded—praise the performers. Whatever took a person's best should be esteemed—let him know it.

Applause has no trouble coming from unselfish, noble minds. It's the self-centered who have trouble praising others because the plaudits are not for them. But as we move out of the inner circle of self, it's easy to move into the outer circle of appreciation.

The deepest principle in human nature is the craving to be appreciated.

—WILLIAM JAMES

Seeing that by these we enjoy great quietness, and that very worthy deeds are done unto this nation by thy providence, we accept it always, and in all places, most noble Felix, with all thankfulness.

—ACTS 24:2,3

Worthy Keepers

Man is obligated to be a keeper. Let's count some ways: (1) Keep himself and his family. This is readily admitted. But even animals do this, at least to some extent. So surely there is more for man to keep. (2) An additional thing is the earth. We cannot have an Eden by exploiting, tearing up and polluting the world God has given us. We are still here, and our posterity shall shortly arrive. What shall they find? (3) We should be keepers of God's Word and hand it down in purity to each generation. (4) It is our duty to keep our fellowman, a brother in need. We must not degenerate into a dog-eat-dog society. Believe me, the bite would be worse than the bark.

May we be worthy keepers!

Never give the wolf the sheep to keep.

—LATIN PROVERB

Am I my brother's keeper?

—GENESIS 4:9

Tardiness Steals Another's Time

The sun is never tardy in rising and setting. God does things on time. And so should we. There are rules that shape our ends, and one of them is punctuality. It is the keeping of a commitment. It shows consideration.

Yet, some people apparently are addicted to being late—always late for everything. It is better to get there early and wait than to get there late and keep the other fellow waiting. It is impolite to waste the other person's time by being late for an appointment. Why should he have to wait? His time is a precious possession, and we have no right to steal it.

Unfaithfulness in keeping an appointment is an act of clear dishonesty. You may as well borrow a person's money as his time.

—HORACE MANN

Do thy diligence to come shortly unto me.

—II TIMOTHY 4:9

Seek to Please

No human can please everybody, but it does add attractiveness and magnetism to have a disposition that seeks to please others. He who pleases is always welcome. When it's possible, therefore, it's smart and winsome to please the other fellow, provided it doesn't displease God. For sure, God's will should come ahead of any person's wishes.

Jesus recognized the priority of God's will in His prayer: "Not my will but thine be done." Basically, this is the best way to please others and to get along with them. Solomon—the wisest human of all times—enunciated this effective principle of human relations: "When a man's ways please the Lord, he maketh even his enemies to be at peace with him" (Proverbs 16:7).

We that live to please must please to live.
—SAMUEL JOHNSON

Let every one of us please his neighbor for his good to edification.
—ROMANS 15:2

Like Drinking Salt Water

G reed has as its slogan get, get, get—never give, give, give. The greedy person seeks fulfillment in life, but the wrong way. It is like drinking salt water; the thirst is never quenched. Greed perverts views and misdirects efforts, which make its victim a pitiful person, a grasping getter but a grievous loser.

When avarice possesses the heart, look out world, trouble is coming. The good-neighbor policy is gone. "Am I my brother's keeper?" is answered in the negative. The helping hand is shriveled. Peace of mind is gone. No matter what's poured into greed, it's never enough, never satisfies. Graspingness and happiness are not in the same person. Greed decomposes the considerate personality and destroys its ability to be happy or productive.

There is no greater disaster than greed.

—LOA TZU
SIXTH CENTURY B.C.

He that is greedy of gain troubleth his own house.
—PROVERBS 15:27

Keeping Secrets

Benjamin Franklin said, "Three may keep a secret if two of them are dead," but we can't kill them; so it's wiser never to tell them. Even then, we still have a problem: We just might talk in our sleep. So the safer course is to have no skeletons in our closets that demand closed doors. For there is one thing sure: Not all mouths will stay closed. However, if we feel that we just have to tell somebody, be very cautious. Never pick a person whose tongue is too long. On the other hand, if we are trusted with a secret, keep it! Never let it slip! Yes, we can keep it. We can keep it by overcoming the urge for the sensational and a moment in the spotlight. There are holier ways to attract attention.

It is wise not to seek a secret and honest not to reveal it.

—BENJAMIN FRANKLIN

A tale bearer revealeth secrets: but he that is of a faithful spirit concealeth the matter.

—PROVERBS 11:13

Sweaty Brows

 A law of God and of nature is work to have. The Creator really knew what He was doing when He appointed man to earn his bread by the sweat of his brow. "No sweat, no sweets." Labor is an antidote to boredom, a protector from evil, a tonic for health, a magnet of interest, and a source of wealth.

Also, honest labor bears a bold countenance that can look the world in the face. Furthermore, the laborer's sleep is sweeter. And just as the woodcutter is known by his chips, the laborer is known by his labors. Man can achieve nothing, fulfil nothing, without labor. It stands between us and our accomplishments.

Let us then be up and doing
With a heart for any fate;
Still achieving, still pursuing,
Learn to labor and to wait.
— Henry Wadsworth Longfellow

In the sweat of thy face shalt thou eat bread, till thou return unto the ground.
— Genesis 3:19

Knock Opens Wide

We need more knocking on doors and less knocking on each other. To engage in the latter is wasted time. To refuse to do the former is wasted opportunity. Not many doors swing open unless they are knocked. Generally speaking, it is as Shakespeare said, "Open, locks, whoever knocks"!

But we can be so busy knocking others that we don't have time to knock on doors. And sometimes we don't knock because we are too blind to see the door. Other times we are unwilling to put forth the exertion to knock. Then we may be tempted to find a perverted kind of ease and satisfaction in knocking the person who does knock.

Where ask is have, where seek is find,
Where knock is open wide.
—Christopher Smart

Ask, and it shall be given you; seek, and ye shall find; knock, and it shall be opened unto you.
—Matthew 7:7

Getting Off the Ground

A ladder is a means by which we get off the ground, but may go down as well as up. In descending, gravity is pulling us down. In ascending, we have to pull up our own weight. We read in the Bible of Jacob's dream of a ladder. It has become a common expression—"Jacob's Ladder."

Today we ascribe to the proposition that God has also given us a ladder by which we rise above the low levels to higher heights. However, some ask, "But Lord, how many steps?" And a hundred other questions. No wonder they don't get off the ground. But here is one encouraging fact for those who climb: As man gets higher, the gravitational pull gets less.

Talk to him of Jacob's ladder, and he would ask the number of steps.

—Douglas Jerrold

As he dreamed, and behold a ladder set up on the earth, and the top of it reached to heaven.

—Genesis 28:12

Better Never Late

T he sun rises and sets on time. The world is run on a clock. Thus he who is late violates both nature's law and man's law. "Better late than never." But "better never late." He who is late for an appointment may rob another of his time. A sophisticated thievery! A minute late may see the plane fly away. In this case, a little too late is much too late.

It takes the same amount of time to do something, whether we are prompt or late. If late, we didn't start soon enough. So if you are inclined to run late, reset your mind's clock and get on time. It will save your nerves and the nerves of others.

He who comes late deserves to eat the leftovers.
—ANONYMOUS

And the king said unto me,...For how long shall thy journey be? And when wilt thou return? So it pleased the king to send me; and I set him a time.
—NEHEMIAH 2:6

Where There Is Honesty

T he world respects an honest man. Since his word is his bond, his signature is superfluous. His plain dealing—free from deceit—makes commerce dependable. His deals are just as open in the dark as they are in the light. He never switches figures from one category to another to conceal data, and he doesn't hide facts in small, unreadable print. He is a revealer of accuracy—not a cover-upper. He never exerts dishonest pressure to secure ill-won money. He never turns himself into a dog to get somebody else's bone.

His honesty is not make-believe. It is his makeup. Call him a square if you wish, but his kind makes the world go round.

An honest man's the noblest work of God.
—ALEXANDER POPE

Provide things honest in the sight of all men.
—ROMANS 12:17

Molders of Man

Hats off to good and worthy teachers: teachers who instruct many, teachers who tutor few, and teachers who teach one on one. They deserve much credit, more than they ordinarily get. Actually, the teacher is the hinge on which education swings. More important than rooms, equipment and textbooks!

The best teachers do more than teach subjects; they teach students and mold lives. As they slant the minds of youth, they tip the world. For we are all what we have been taught—one way or another; and as man turns, so turns the world. So it is appropriate that we extol meritorious teachers. They are like candles; as they consume themselves, they light others—and the world.

A teacher affects eternity; he can never tell where his influence stops.
                              —HENRY BROOKS ADAMS

Ye have need that one teach you.
                              —HEBREWS 5:12

World of Effort

A few things come to us without effort, like old age; but getting the most out of old age or any age requires effort—spiritual, mental and physical. The never-sweats never get. Inspiration needs to be mixed with perspiration. See the people on the mountain peak; they got there through effort. Now look at the people at the lower levels who were not willing to expend the energy to climb; they have no victory, no jubilation.

Whether talent is big or little, let each of us so live that he can say at the end of the journey, "I have put forth the best effort I could." What seems impossible to the halfhearted is accomplished by the dedicated, unrelenting efforts of others.

Good luck favors effort.

—ANONYMOUS

Master, we have toiled all the night.

—LUKE 5:5

Two Faces

A person may refine his hypocrisy to the nth degree, but it still adds up to two faces, and sooner or later the world recognizes both. We only fool ourselves when we put on the masks of hypocrisy and masquerade as people we're not. Let's put away pretense. Let's be what we really are. Jesus tried to get this lesson over to the pious, pretending Pharisees. He likened them to "whited sepulchers, which indeed appear beautiful outward, but are within full of dead men's bones" (Matthew 23:27).

There are hypocrites everywhere: church, shop, school, lodge, office, home, everywhere on earth. But in the same realms there are many, many sincere and true people. Actually, the hypocrite compliments the exemplary life by being an imitator of it. His duplicity testifies to what a person should be, though he's not.

O what may a man within him hide,
Though angel on the outward side.
—WILLIAM SHAKESPEARE

Beware of false prophets, which come to you in sheep's clothing, but inwardly they are ravening wolves.
—MATTHEW 7:15

Mother of Poverty

Idle people have the least leisure and the most trouble. For their idleness gives them an emptiness which dehydrates and shrivels the soul. It's the mother of poverty and the father of beggary. It's the field of vice and the root of mischief. It's the devil's workshop, and he works it day and night.

It's amusing how ridiculous the idler becomes in excusing his slothfulness. The Bible tells of one who said that he couldn't go to work because there was a lion out there. To get out of work, loafers make ferocious lions out of friendly kittens. But it still remains—the surest way to be nothing is to do nothing.

For Satan finds some mischief still
  For idle hands to do.

—Isaac Watts

Drowsiness shall clothe a man with rags.

—Proverbs 23:21

Let God Handle It

What wrongs are committed in the name of repayment of wrongs! Black as the night. Hot as blazes. Vengeance can be perpetrated with such ignorance of facts, perversion of justice and show of aggrandizement. That is why it is better to let God take care of it.

Slaves of vengeance are never free. Locked in a pitiful cell of hate and spite, they have denied themselves the freer and happier life.

If the get-eveners could see the future, they would act with more restraint. For what is vindictively done adds fuel to the fire, and soon there is a conflagration out of control. Not tame justice! Just wild injustice! And as the retaliation compounds, it gets more difficult to get even because each time it lowers the perpetrator. There is no way to win. Because, in settling the score, a higher tally does not make one a winner.

For revenge is always the delight of a mean spirit, of a weak and petty mind!
—DECIMUS JUNIUS JUVENAL

Vengeance belongeth unto me, I will recompense, saith the Lord.
—HEBREWS 10:30

The Right Job

Every able person needs a job—even the retired who can devote free time to good works. It is exhilarating to be on a job that means more than money.

Here are some guidelines for the best job: One for which a person is fitted. One that he enjoys. Maximizes his talents. Contributes to the welfare of our society. Is challenging. Has opportunities for advancement. Pays enough to support the worker's needs. When these conditions are met, the work becomes a form of play. Blessed is the person who finds such a job. And he who does the best he can, whether the job is considered great or small, will fill his days with invigoration and zest.

The right people in the right jobs.
—OTTO VON BISMARCK

And with him was Aholiab—an engraver, and a cunning workman, and an embroiderer in blue, and in purple, and in scarlet, and in fine linen.
—EXODUS 38:23

Imperfection Walks the Earth

Imperfection—now that's a field in which man stars. The very greatest men have shown great faults, faults that seemed to be all the greater in contrast with their shining virtues. Noah, Abraham, David, Solomon and Peter are but a few of the names that adorn the pages of excellence whose lives were blotched with imperfections.

The loftiest people of highest pursuits, while racked with imperfection, are the pursuers of perfection. Things and lives get better only as imperfections are overcome. As long as we recognize our flaws and pray and work to mend them, we're making progress on the high road.

How few there are who have courage enough to own their faults, or resolution enough to mend them.

—BENJAMIN FRANKLIN

Let us go on unto perfection.

—HEBREWS 6:1

Anger or Danger

Anger in ourselves is classified as a conscientious emotion that got triggered; but in others it is seen as an explosive hothead with a short fuse. Actually, at times each can be true. Clearly, anger—irritation, vexation, displeasure, resentment—is not necessarily bad because it can be righteous indignation and deep feeling against wrong.

But when not handled properly, anger is just one letter short of danger. It's a primary risk factor in cardiovascular disease. Furthermore, it's a killer of success and knocks many off the upward ladder. If the temper boils over, then the hothead is in hot water, and the heat affects the normal function of the brain. Keep cool!

Anger, if not restrained, is frequently more hurtful to us than the injury that it provokes.
—SENECA
(8 B.C.-A.D. 65)

Be ye angry, and sin not: let not the sun go down upon your wrath.
—EPHESIANS 4:26

No Broken Crutches

One of the most helpful benefits of man is independence. Expecting the other fellow to support us is like leaning on a broken crutch. Too much dependence stunts development and takes away freedom. It's like being in jail. There, people have three meals a day but no independence, no freedom and no dignity. The free lunch becomes a servitude.

Nothing can be more upgrading and stature-building than for us, with God's help, to support ourselves by our own exertions. While it is good for us to stand on our own feet, it's not wise never to lean on another. We live in a world of interrelations in which we need each other. So be dependently independent.

Every tub must stand upon its bottom.
—CHARLES MACKLIN

The eyes of servants look unto the hand of their masters.
—PSALM 123:2

Flowers or Thistles

There is as much difference between the industrious life and the slothful life as there is between a beautiful flower garden and a patch of thorns and thistles. One, the fruit of industry; the other, the result of indolence.

The industrious person and the lethargic person pursue different courses, and it is only natural that their destinies are different. Very little is ever attained without the application of one's abilities and the seizing of one's opportunities. The hard-working person puts his shoulder to the wheel and turns it into a wheel of fortune, and he keeps it lubricated with his own elbow grease. This is why things hum for him.

Life without industry is guilt.

—JOHN RUSKIN

And the man Jeroboam was a mighty man of valour: and Solomon seeing the young man that he was industrious, he made him ruler over all the charge of the house of Joseph.

—I KINGS 11:28

Self-made Halos Are Blinding

Humility is much more helpful than pride and much more acceptable to the public. Pride causes a person to stand in his own way and block his own progress. It won't let him climb up because he thinks he's already up. The tragedy is that he will never get to the top because he has too much pride to start at the bottom. He won't sell in the market because he has inflated his value. The public is not deceived by haughtiness, not even the haughtiness of pretending to be humble.

Humility, however, is not drooping beneath one's stature; but neither is it standing on stilts. While it is not blind to ability, it is dependent on God and man. That's humility.

After crosses and losses men grow humbler and wiser.

—BENJAMIN FRANKLIN

For whosoever exalteth himself shall be abased; and he that humbleth himself shall be exalted.

—LUKE 4:11

Beauty of Youth

Young people lack experience but not intelligence. Impulsive, but at least there is an aggressive spirit. Unafraid, which can lead to dangerous situations; but again, they are not weighted down with fear. Inquisitive? Yes. They are not status quoers. They want to know what we're going to do about a world that aches with self-inflicted pain. Their remedy may be simplistic, nevertheless it shows an urge to apply some treatment. Fair and unprejudiced, just give them the truth and they will handle it properly.

All they need is guidance, example, discipline, praise, a sense of right, and a consciousness of God. They need it now. Their light can either gleam or go out.

Happy is this, she is not yet so old
But she may learn.

—WILLIAM SHAKESPEARE

Remember now thy Creator in the days of thy youth.

—ECCLESIASTES 12:1

Calmness in Vexations

Mind is stronger than vexation. An annoyance shall disturb us only if we permit it. So let us be too big and too disciplined to be vexed by small matters or testy circumstances. Of course, a gnat can be very annoying, but we are too rational to be overwhelmed by it. The same sanity should be exercised in handling all unpleasantries, irritations and harassments.

We should give ourselves a mental tranquilizer whereby we save ourselves from tattered nerves. Then, as we meet our problems in complete control of ourselves, strengthened with calmness and resoluteness, we find the solutions easier.

Remember to preserve a calm soul amid difficulties.

—HORACE
(65-8 B.C.)

For whom a man is overcome, of the same is he brought in bondage.

—II PETER 2:19

No Ordinary Bird

D on't be a parrot; be a thinker. This makes you no ordinary bird. A distinction of man is the ability to think. There is no future in just squawking like a parrot; devoid of thinking, he remains caged. The rungs on the success ladder are made of brains; and the more they are exercised in thinking, the higher the person climbs. It is rashness that pulls the ladder out from under us. Then the crash. We hadn't been thinking.

No matter how bleak our situation may look, there is still hope if we take time to do some analytical thinking. It is thinking that turns supposed hopelessness into realistic hope. Four things are very essential: Be honest. Get to the bottom of the matter. Be willing to listen. Figure out a course of action. THINK!

The most necessary task of civilization is to teach man how to think.

—THOMAS A. EDISON

How think ye?

—MATTHEW 18:12

Questions and Answers

To "beg the question" is not to answer it. Yet every question doesn't deserve an answer. Foolish and unlearned questions should be avoided for they engender strife. And concerning God, we don't need a question, just a period.

However, there are many proper questions we need to ask in facing the affairs and issues of life. Three especially, according to John Lubbock: "Is it right or wrong? Is it true or false? Is it beautiful or ugly?" When we enlarge on these three by asking who? when? what? which? how? where? and why? it gives us a broader insight. It is better to ask a question than to later regret that we didn't.

No question is ever settled until it is settled right.

—ELLA WHEELER WILCOX

And when the queen of Sheba heard of the fame of Solomon concerning the name of the Lord, she came to prove him with hard questions.

—I KINGS 10:1

Earned Rest

Rest is not idleness. Neither is quitting idleness; it's only the cessation of effort to renew strength for a continuation of the project. A wise intermission! For no runner can run all the time, no fighter can fight all the time, and no worker can work all the time.

Both mind and muscle require rest. Its value, however, is found in its contrast and proportion. There can be too much work. There can be too much rest. Blessed are they who know when to do each and in its proper amount.

The thing that makes rest so delightful is its coming after hard work. Truly, one of the attractions of heaven is that there "the weary are at rest."

Work, and your house shall be duly fed:
Work, and rest shall be won.

—ALICE CARY

Wash your feet, and rest yourselves under the tree.

—GENESIS 18:4

The Good Fight

To be a Christian is to be a fighter—the right kind and in the right ways. For there rages in the world a ceaseless conflict between truth and error, good and evil, love and hate, helpfulness and exploitation, freedom and despotism. Indeed, conviction won't let a person be neutral in the strife.

All evil has to do to prevail is for the righteous to do nothing. There is such a thing as one's being too complacent to fight; and another, too cowardly. It may be expedient to retreat today, but only to close ranks and fight tomorrow. For life is one constant struggle.

No one conquers who doesn't fight.

—GABRIEL BIEL

Put on the whole armor of God, that ye may be able to stand against the wiles of the devil. For we wrestle not against flesh and blood, but against principalities, against powers, against the rulers of the darkness of this world, against spiritual wickedness in high places.

—EPHESIANS 6:11,12

Fun Spices Life

T he person too serious to relax and have a little fun may be courting disaster—maybe a breakdown, or at least ineffectiveness. Life was meant to be a delightful pilgrimage, not an unkind existence of grimness or boredom or misery.

To have fun, however, we have to have the right circumstances. It is as Will Rogers said, "Spinning a rope's a lot of fun—provided your neck ain't in it." Now, that's where we come in. It's left up to us to make or alter the circumstances. It's easy for children to have fun, but adults have to do more to get it.

Fun is like insurance: the older you get, the more it costs.

—KIN HUBBARD

Then I commended mirth, because a man hath no better thing under the sun, than to eat, and to drink, and to be merry.

—ECCLESIASTES 8:15

A Little Leaven

Influence is one of the most powerful, far-reaching forces in all the world. Sometimes it is so subtle that people hardly know they are being affected. All of us have at least some influence, good or bad. Having this far-reaching power, it behooves us to exercise the wholesome influence. In this manner, little by little, we make the world better. The sermons we live have more impact than the ones we preach. In leaving our footprints on the sands of time, we can either leave the marks of a heel that will make us a heel or the marks of a sole that will save a soul.

The blossom cannot tell what becomes of its odor; and no man can tell what becomes of his influence.

—HENRY WARD BEECHER

Know ye not that a little leaven leaveneth the whole lump?

—I CORINTHIANS 5:6

Good News

The word gospel literally means good news. The gospel of Christ is the good news of Christ and all that pertains to His plan to save and bless man. It is good news for the sin-cursed that need forgiveness, for the confounded that need direction, for the weary that need strength, for the brokenhearted that need comfort, and for the forlorn that need hope.

It is something to believe. Something to obey. Something to preach. And something to love. In living it, we present to the world the Fifth Gospel, the examples of our lives.

The Gospels of Matthew, Mark, Luke and John,
Are read by more than a few,
But the one that is most read and commented on
Is the gospel according to you.

—ANONYMOUS

We...suffer all things, lest we should hinder the gospel of Christ.

—I CORINTHIANS 9:12

Striving for Excellence

E xcellence is a thing for which we should strive. Reach for the stars. It should be our goal in character, style, manners, employment, and in our relationship with God and man.

It is the way to get ahead. If we do things better than others, we shall rise above them. The plaudits go to those who excel. The world beats a path to their door.

However, there is a price. God has put effort before excellence, time to bring it to maturity, and stability to give it substance. "Unstable as water, thou shalt not excel" (Genesis 49:4).

It is a wretched taste to be gratified with mediocrity when the excellent lies before us.
—ISAAC D'ISRAELI

Seek that ye may excel....
—I CORINTHIANS 14:12

From Different Molds

Since all humans were not made from the same mold, we have individuality. Therefore, it is right for each individual to live on the individual basis: individual ability, individual brains, individual will and individual energy. Certainly this does not bar improvement, but it must be done on the basis whereby each remains himself—not somebody he's not, not a counterfeit.

Any government concept that would lessen individuality in the hope of strengthening the whole society would actually enfeeble and degrade the whole. Individuality—with its individual liberties, potentials and opportunities—must ever be the intent of government.

We are facing a great danger today—the loss of our individuality. It is besieged on all sides by pressures to conform.

—ELEANOR ROOSEVELT

So then every one of us shall give account of himself to God.

—ROMANS 14:12

Morning of Hope

Here is what hope is: Hope is believing—trusts in the promises of the Bible and makes them a part of life. Hope is visionary—sees beyond the present and looks to the future. Hope is a waking dream—optimism takes over and anticipates. Hope is the mainspring of life—keeps life's wheels turning. Hope is stabilizing—keeps the heart from sinking and the hands from folding. Hope is tireless—defies exhaustion and keeps going. Hope is musical—provides a melody for the soul when grief or difficulties come. Hope is medicinal—the most potent tonic.

Have hope. Though clouds environ now,
  And gladness hides her face in scorn,
Put thou the shadow from thy brow—
    No night but hath its morn.
    —JOHANN CHRISTOPHER FRIEDRICH VON SCHILLER

For to him that is joined to all the living there is hope.

—ECCLESIASTES 9:4

The Highest Flattery

Man is an imitative creature. It begins early. A child learns to talk and walk by listening to and looking at its parents. But he also learns to limp by looking at the lame and to squint by looking at the cross-eyed.

So—first, when you start to imitate be certain the pattern is excellent. Second, in imitating another be sure you end up as yourself, not a counterfeit. Third, never be content to rise only to the model's level, for this might doom you to a level beneath your ability.

Indeed, imitation is the highest flattery; so when you are imitated, feel complimented.

There is much difference between imitating a good man and counterfeiting him.

—BENJAMIN FRANKLIN

Ye have us for an example.

—PHILIPPIANS 3:17

Stepping Upward

Moving upward is only man's distinctive trait, not God's, not beasts'; God is as high as high, and beasts are low to remain there, content to eat and whisk flies. But man was meant to climb, and he can if he has the upward look and the determination to raise himself above where he stands.

Up! For genius dies and folly lives when there is no upward exertion. Then what might have risen never gets off the ground, just lingers and limps in dusty commonness. Life has its ups and downs: When down, get up; when up, move up. Higher, there is more room, not so crowded.

Up, lad: when the journey's over
There'll be time enough to sleep.
—ALFRED EDWARD HOUSMAN

And they rose up early in the morning, and got them into the top of the mountain.
—NUMBERS 14:40

Careful Judging

I t is so easy to err in judging: (1) Having only a fragment of information leads to untrue judgments. We are reminded of the blind man who erred in assuming an elephant is like a tree because all he felt was the elephant's leg. (2) Many things are not what they seen and can be perceived in a false light. (3) One may allow his own wishes to affect verdicts. He sees what he wants to see. (4) Outward appearances can be so deceptive.

Therefore, judge adversely only when necessary, with full knowledge, with utmost fairness, with a leaning toward mercy, and with a consideration of self in similar circumstances.

Nor is the people's judgment always true:
The most may err as grossly as the few.
—JOHN DRYDEN

Judge not, that ye be not judged.
—MATTHEW 7:1

Who Is the Boss?

N ot everybody can be boss. No person can be a law unto himself. And most of all, no human can be God. Hence, adherence—obeying laws and following rules—is essential to a productive life and a solid society.

There are the civil laws of man and the divine laws of God. Both demand adherence. However, if the keeping of man's laws should violate the keeping of God's laws, then it leaves no choice but to give God priority and obey Him.

Furthermore, there are the rules, regulations, customs and niceties in our society that require compliance lest we stigmatize ourselves as rebellious oddballs, which hardship we should not have to suffer except in an instance of conscience's sake. There is no glory in being different for difference's sake.

The superior man...what is right he will follow.
—CONFUCIUS
(551-479 B.C.)

And whosoever shall compel thee to go a mile, go with him twain.
—MATTHEW 5:41

Sugar Instead of Vinegar

Tact is not Tack, which pricks, nor Attack, which assails. Rather, it is T-A-C-T.

T—ouch or feeling that reaches out.

A—djustment that regulates itself to the circumstances rather than follow set, inflexible approaches.

C—arefulness that is circumspect, guarded, thoughtful and judicious.

T—emperament that exemplifies a tempered disposition, not easily heated, filled with composure, calmness and tenderness.

Additionally, it is knowing how far to go; also, a willingness to hear many things we have already heard. Summed up, it is feeding sugar instead of vinegar.

Tact is after all a kind of mind-reading.
—SARAH ORNE JEWETT

There is that speaketh like the piercings of a sword: but the tongue of the wise is health.
—PROVERBS 12:18

Simple Joys

Joy is never found by those who seek it too hard. They come up with bewildering disappointment or glossy superficiality, not the real.

Observation tells us that joy is more apt to be found in simple things—lovely family, plain home, romp of children, coffee brewing, bread baking, singing kettle, fresh-cut rose in a vase, companionship that affords acceptance and appreciation, friendly handshake, performance of duties, simple faith, supportive hope, abiding love, clear conscience, walking with God and casting your burdens on Him.

People look for joy in expensive domains when actually it can be found on free, help-yourself counters.

My fair son!
My life, my joy, my food, my all the world.
—WILLIAM SHAKESPEARE

Weeping may endure for a night, but joy cometh in the morning.
—PSALM 30:5

Golden Eggs

There are many investments: in knowledge, in health, in friendship, in materials, and also in heaven itself. Jesus said of the latter, "But lay up for yourselves treasures in heaven" (Matthew 6:20). At a time when so many banks are going under, it is assuring to know that the bank of heaven shall never default.

An investment in self (knowledge, health and soul) is surely better than hoarding a dollar which may never do you any good.

A wise investment is like a goose that lays golden eggs. Before making an investment in materials, think all relevant matters through: advantages versus disadvantages, risks versus rewards, and the present versus the future. Then sleep on it before you decide.

A fool and his money are soon parted.
—AUTHOR UNKNOWN
(CURRENT SAYING SINCE THE 16TH CENTURY.)

Thou oughtest therefore to have put my money to the exchangers.
—MATTHEW 25:27

Everyday Heroes

The word *heroism* is used to describe daring deeds on battlefields and dangerous exploits in blood-curdling crises.

However, it aptly pictures millions in the everyday walks of life. The person who faces what he must and fights the daily battles with an unconquerable spirit is a hero—crown him. The woman who died for her child is a heroine, but so is she who gives her life day by day to see her baby blossom into maturity—crown her. The person who leads a crowd in difficult times is a hero, but so is the person who has the bravery to break with the crowd and stand alone in his convictions—crown him. He who died for his faith is a hero, but so is he who lives it—crown him.

Blessed are they who die for God,
  And earn the martyr's crown of light;
Yet he who lives for God may be
  A greater conqueror in His sight.
                                    —ANONYMOUS

Be of good courage, and he shall strengthen your heart, all ye that hope in the Lord.
                                    —PSALM 31:24

Launch Out

I nitiative contains the letter "I" three times. Not once does it have the letter "U." In my success, what "I" do is three times as vital as what "U" do.

All successful people have initiative. They are more than thinkers; they are doers, performers, hard workers. The person who takes the initiative can always find plenty to do. His willingness to tackle a job gets things done and rewards him. But the person who stands around with his hands in his pockets never fills them with much else.

We have machines to move mountains, but what moves machines? People. People with initiative.

Up! mind thine own aim, and God speed the mark!

—RALPH WALDO EMERSON

Jacob said unto his sons, why do ye look one upon another?

—GENESIS 42:1

Help Me

One of the most repeated words is "help"—"help me." It comes from a million voices across the land: from playrooms, classrooms, assembly lines, unemployment offices, military ranks, sick rooms, flower-decked graves, hovels, mansions and church altars. It shows the insufficiency of man.

Every little helps. Too much assistance, however, may not help. The most effective way to help anybody is to help him to help himself. While God is the best helper, He wants a little effort from man to help himself. God gives the corn, but He wants us to shell it.

He that is thy friend indeed,
He will help thee in thy need.
—RICHARD BARNFIELD

They helped every one his neighbor; and every one said to his brother, Be of good courage.
—ISAIAH 41:6

Priceless Comfort

"Thy rod and thy staff they comfort me." This is from the beautiful and immortal Twenty-third Psalm. Comfort from the Shepherd's rod, which provides guidance and discipline. Comfort from the Shepherd's staff, a source of strength upon which man may lean in any crisis, weakness, affliction or anguish, both bodily and spiritual.

The most untenable and uncomfortable position of any person is to live apart from God's rod and staff and to doubt His care. This leaves an empty feeling with a forlorn outlook. But living with faith in the Lord's goodness forbids dismay and makes for repose—"he maketh me to lie down in green pastures."

Now, God be prais'd, that to believing souls
Gives light in darkness, comfort in despair.
—WILLIAM SHAKESPEARE

The Lord is my shepherd; I shall not want.
—PSALM 23:1

Direct My Steps

An educated mind, a humble spirit and an honest heart—as important as they are—are still not enough to guide man. Much education does not teach intelligence, nor do good intentions always put us on the right course.

More is needed. Man still needs to tap a perception smarter than his, a wisdom wiser than his, and a strength stronger than his. We have needs this earth cannot supply. Our modern society has tried every sort of a guide except one, and it's about time we were getting back to it: the Bible. It "is a lamp unto my feet, and a light unto my path." Let's give it a chance.

The direction in which education starts a man will determine his future life.

—PLATO
(428-348 B.C.)

O Lord, I know that the way of man is not in himself: it is not in man that walketh to direct his steps.

—JEREMIAH 10:23

A Time to Laugh

The laughter of a fool is as Solomon stated, like "the crackling of thorns under a pot." If it's the silly giggling of a vacant mind, it's meaningless. If it comes from a sorrowful heart, it's an effort to be brave and is only superficial. But if it's the natural reaction to a situation wrought with peace, merriment or comedy, it's a delightful experience, a relaxer for nerves, a tonic for health and a magnetism that attracts others.

To know when to laugh is as important as the act itself. If ill-timed, it's embarrassing. If properly timed, it's dynamic.

We are all here for a spell. Get all the good laughs you can.

—WILL ROGERS

Therefore Sarah laughed within herself, saying, After I am waxed old shall I have pleasure, my lord being old also?

—GENESIS 18:12

Encourage Me

When we are in the Valley of Depression, we need encouragement to climb the Mount of Optimism beside it. They are not far apart.

Encouragement can be oxygen for a fainting heart and vitamins for a struggling life. Correction is helpful, but sometimes encouragement is more helpful. It brings out the best in most people. And the one who gives it is always welcome. Moreover, it is self-protection, protects the encourager from gloom by permitting him to walk in the very sunshine he turns on for others.

My day takes on a brand-new zest,
Your gift of praising brings my best,
Revives my spirit, flings it high;
For God loves praise, and so do I.
—AUTHOR UNKNOWN

So the carpenter encouraged the goldsmith, and he that smootheth with the hammer him that smote the anvil....
—ISAIAH 41:7

When Knowledge Abounds

The greatest knowledge is to know God. The second is to know self. Knowledge is riches. The person of knowledge possesses a treasure more precious than gold. Stock markets can tumble and depressions can bankrupt, but the riches of knowledge remain.

However, there can be pitfalls in knowledge. While it humbles great men, it puffs up little ones. Furthermore, as Alexander Pope stated, "A little learning is a dangerous thing." Half knowledge is more destructive than whole ignorance. Our welfare necessitates that we ascertain full knowledge. For the first requirement to do better is to know better.

Consider your origin; you were not born to live like brutes, but to follow virtue and knowledge.
—DANTE

Every prudent man dealeth with knowledge: but a fool layeth open his folly.
—PROVERBS 13:16

True Wealth

Views of wealth can be highly prejudiced: from those who have none and never expect any, and from those who have much and very little else. The most credible and sensible view, however, is expressed in the Bible. It tells us that God provided a world of blessings for the benefit of man. This is "his portion," "his birthright." Man was meant to prosper.

To have wealth, however, and not use it makes its owner no richer than a poor man; and to love it and idolize it makes him poorer than a pauper. Since true wealth is not measured in materials, then there are the rich poor people and the poor rich people. How much better it is to be rich rich—rich spiritually and materially! It can be. Many in the Bible were.

Large was his wealth, but larger was his heart.
—JOHN DRYDEN

But thou shalt remember the Lord thy God: for it is he that giveth thee power to get wealth....
—DEUTERONOMY 8:18

For Justice to Be Just

Justice is very demanding. Justice is not justice if it is a rule made just for us. If it follows a double standard. If it is measured by a temporary standard. If it is a respecter of persons. If it is based on expediency. If it spares the bad. If it corrupts the good. If it sees what it wants to see. If it is extended to the accuser but denied the accused or vice versa. If it strains at a gnat and swallows a camel. And if it is delayed too long.

While most of us plead for justice, our greater need is mercy. This is certainly true in our relationship with God. We want clemency rather than our due.

Nothing can be honorable where justice is absent.

—CICERO
(106-43 B.C.)

For I know him, that he will command his children and his household after him, and they shall keep the way of the Lord, to do justice and judgment....

—GENESIS 18:19

Clothed in Honor

We should render honor to whom honor is due, but only to the ones to whom it is due. The wise man Solomon stated, "Honor is not seemly for a fool." Very incongruous! Giving honor to an unworthy person is like putting a diamond in a pig's snout. Incompatible. The diamond flashes but not the pig.

Others can build up our reputation—what people think of us—but we and we alone are the makers of our honor. It is like a battlefield commission; it must be earned in the strife of conflict. Or like an honorary doctorate; it must be earned in the stress of life.

When faith is lost, when honor dies,
The man is dead.
—JOHN GREENLEAF WHITTIER

Strength and honor are her clothing....
—PROVERBS 31:25

The Difference of Indifference

Indifference or difference: Which shall it be? For it makes a difference! WHEN parents use television sets for baby-sitters with no concern for the kind of pictures and programs...WHEN parents never bother about the crowd their children run with...WHEN narcotics are used to make merchandise of people...WHEN jail attendance is growing faster than church attendance... WHEN truthfulness and honesty are only trivial matters of convenience...WHEN idleness is honored with payouts...WHEN responsibility is disregarded...WHEN God is forgotten except in times of illness and death...THEN it is time for an awakening in this nation.

At length the morn and cold indifference came.
—NICHOLAS ROWE

And they said, What is that to us?
—MATTHEW 27:4

Make Up Your Mind

M ake up your mind. This moving world won't wait for you. Those who hesitate are left behind. In waiting too long to begin, it becomes too late. Opportunity is lost. Indecision is the chief architect of air castles. The major stifler of business. And the chief cause of military defeat.

Decide, but not rashly. Take time to deliberate and devise the best way; and after that, it's time for action. Get with it. Some who have hesitated to line up with God, assuring themselves that they still had the eleventh hour, have died at ten-fifty. Life will not long tolerate indecision. The clock keeps ticking.

I am at war 'twixt will and will not.
—WILLIAM SHAKESPEARE

How long halt ye between two opinions?
—I KINGS 18:21

Tried by Fire

To recognize that hardship to some degree is sure to come sooner or later is not pessimistic, just realistic. Don't try to run from it when it strikes. Running away just takes us out of the running.

It is better to keep ourselves so positioned that when we get kicked, we get kicked forward. The blows show the stuff we're made of. Hardship has revealed many a hero; the heroic quality was there all the time, but it took the testing to bring it out and to develop it. The hardiest trees are those that have withstood wind and tempest in open ground, not those in hothouses. So it is of man.

Gold is tried by fire, brave men by adversity.
—SENECA
(8 B.C.-A.D. 65)

That the trial of your faith, being much more precious than of gold that perisheth, though it be tried with fire, might be found unto praise and honor and glory....
—II PETER 1:7

Make Haste Slowly

In our hurry and fret we have become counterproductive. We have allowed haste to chase us to no avail. We have missed the security of correctness, the safety of prudence, the production of excellence, and the calmness of walking and talking with God.

Indeed, this essay is no defense of laziness and slowness, but rather an appeal, as Augustus Caesar stated, to "make haste slowly." Never move faster than prudence allows, for haste trips on its own heels. Hasty climbers are more apt to fall. Hasty eating may choke the diner. And hasty people don't make good midwives. It just takes time for some occurrences and accomplishments.

Take time for all things: great haste makes great waste.

—BENJAMIN FRANKLIN

The thoughts of the diligent tend only to plenteousness; but of every one that is hasty only to want.

—PROVERBS 21:5

Count on Me

One of the finest compliments ever spoken is, "You can count on him." It's worth much to have the reputation that you will not let another down. That's coming through when the going is rough. In fair weather and foul. That's character. That's trustworthiness.

No person counts much who can't be counted on. A dependable person with average ability is much more valuable than a wavering genius. This is one value within the reach of all. Each can set his heart, stiffen his backbone, and be true to the trust.

He was a gentleman on whom I built an absolute trust.

—WILLIAM SHAKESPEARE

Yet I supposed it necessary to send to you Epaphroditus, my brother, and companion in labour.... Because for the work of Christ he was nigh unto death, not regarding his life, to supply your lack of service toward me.

—PHILIPPIANS 2:25-30

Heaven Holds All

Heaven is a place where death is no more, tears are wiped away and troubles never come. It is too necessary not to be true! If there is no other life, if this earthly existence is all there is for man, then the Creator's plan never accomplishes one permanent thing and ends in colossal failure.

It is just as easy for God to give heaven as it was to give earth. The very word God transcends human limitations and gives eternal hope.

The prices we pay to reach heaven are cheap, whatever they cost. The best real estate deal any person can make is to secure a promissory deed to a mansion in the Promised Land.

Earth holds no treasures but perish with using,
However precious they be;
Yet there's a country to which I am going:
Heaven holds all to me.

—TILLIT S. TEDDLIE

In my Father's house are many mansions....

—JOHN 14:2

Small Packages

Take "I" out of some people's vocabulary and it would almost silence them. The other fellow has eyes, too—eyes that see the "I's" and is not impressed. An exaggerated sense of self-importance complicates human relations. It is difficult for two persons to associate together when one of them thinks the whole world revolves around him and that nothing is important except what he says. The other party usually regards such chatter too low to be elevating.

But there is one thing we can say for the egotist: He just cannot tolerate egotism. However, what he does not like in others he fails to see in himself.

When a person is wrapped up in himself, he makes a pretty small package.

—JOHN RUSKIN

A man's pride shall bring him low: but honor shall uphold the humble in spirit.

—PROVERBS 29:23

Hesitation Falters Life

Many a *what could be* hesitates and becomes a *what might have been,* the victim of reluctance. If we wait until there is no danger in traveling, we will be left behind. Oftentimes when the light is green, we're afraid to move for fear it may turn red.

Certainly we should take time to think a matter through, but too much time—hesitation—can allow the opportunity to pass us by. Too many people wait for the more opportune time, which never comes. There is no success in waiting and folding our hands. When the apple reddens, it's time to pick. All progress is in deciding and rolling up our sleeves.

Who hesitate and falter life away,
And lose tomorrow the ground won today.
—MATTHEW ARNOLD

But the man would not tarry that night, but he rose up and departed....
—JUDGES 19:10

Shine On

T his is what we all should try to be: light. We need to shine, and the world needs the light. It is a symbol of openness, truth, guidance, cheerfulness, sustenance and influence. The fewer lights we have, the more benighted our world becomes. So the problems stemming from a dark world can be overcome by more lights.

Shine! Give off cool light. Not hot heat. Not lightning—not a momentary flash and a roar of thunder. Shine steadily—not just twinkle. Shine openly. Don't hide your light under a bushel. Some poor, struggling seaman may need your light to make the harbor.

More light.

—JOHN WOLFGANG VON GOETHE
(HIS LAST WORDS.)

...shine as lights in the world....

—PHILIPPIANS 2:15

Busy Bee

It is good to keep busy, provided one is busy with productive matters. The person on a treadmill or merry-go-round is busy, but he doesn't get anywhere. For busyness to be profitable, it must be judiciously and constructively directed.

We can be so absorbed with the lesser concerns that we have no time for the bigger values. Much ado about very little. In that case, real living is brought to a halt. It reminds us of the rush hour on the freeway when traffic is almost at a standstill. And those accidents—they suggest that one never gets too busy to attend his own funeral. Idleness is hurtful. Excessive busyness is also hurtful. Be temperate.

How doth the little busy bee
Improve each shining hour,
And gather honey all the day
From every opening flower!

—ISAAC WATTS

And as thy servant was busy here and there, he was gone.

—I KINGS 20:40

Cool Heads

What does calmness show? It manifests a strong personality in harmony with itself and at peace with its ideals. Indeed, there can be no self-composure if one is fighting a battle within himself; it has to be won, and there can be no smooth sailing until the tempest within is quieted. Furthermore, it signifies faith, confidence and the hope that difficulties will work out satisfactorily.

Keep your thinking clear if you would have peaceful days ahead. Stay calm. The human brain doesn't run on hot steam that blows the top. Cool heads are more efficient than hot ones. Steady your nerves. For the best of you is needed to respond whenever and wherever discordant circumstances arise.

Remember to preserve a calm soul amid difficulties.

—HORACE
(65-8 B.C.)

...even the ornament of a meek and quiet spirit, which is in the sight of God of great price.

—I PETER 3:4

You Can

Don't listen to the "can'ters" who say a thing can't be done. It just may be they can't do it, not you. With their brains in negative gear, we shouldn't expect them to do it. When a person says "I can't," he bids himself to stand still while success moves on and leaves him behind.

The Moving Finger of History records successes and failures, and in writing them it separates the "I caners" from the "I can'ters." And all the tears of unaccomplishment won't wash out one word, but a change of mind—"I can"—can alter the future. Having broken the iron shackles of laziness and fear, there is the precious freedom to perform, to attain. You can!

It is now almost my sole rule of life to clear myself of can'ts and formulas.

—THOMAS CARLYLE

Jesus said unto him, If thou canst believe, all things are possible to him that believeth.

—MARK 9:23

Courage to Stand

Any coward can applaud right, but it takes courage to stand for it. The grins of mockery, the censorship of ridicule, and the loss of popularity can make cowards out of otherwise valiant people. Some can face guns easier than they can face grins.

Cultivate courage by devotion to conscientious principles, commitment to duty, assessment of what really counts in the end, and trust in God for help and power.

Stick with honor to be a winner. Let the opposition strike; and when they are gone, truth and right shall still be living.

Wealth lost, something lost; honor lost, much lost; courage lost, all lost.
—JOHANN WOLFGANG VON GOETHE

Be strong and of a good courage, fear not, nor be afraid of them: for the Lord thy God, he it is that doth go with thee; he will not fail thee, nor forsake thee.
—DEUTERONOMY 31:6

Crosses Into Ladders

You have a cross to bear. Everyone does. Just different kinds and different weights. It is not always possible to live life the way we would like it to be. We have to face the problems that exist. That's reality. And reality sometimes means crosses to bear.

If we can't honorably eliminate the crosses, then the next-best thing is to ask God to give us strength to bear them and to use them. They can be made into ladders whereby we rise to greater heights. Then at the higher altitude, we are able to see what we never saw from beneath. This helps to take the fret out of it.

To fret thy soul with crosses and with cares;
To eat thy heart through comfortless despairs.
— EDMUND SPENCER

...and the month which was turned unto them from sorrow to joy, and from mourning into a good day: that they should make them days of feasting and joy....
— ESTHER 9:22

Gold or Brass

It is galling to be deceived, and it's even worse to be duped by self. This is the blindest blindness and the most impostrous impostor.

In hope of making a catch, we can hide the hook with deceptive bait, but there are always some big fish out there that will pull us in. Then which one was deceived? It is foolhardy for us to think that we are more clever than all the others. We cannot cry gold and sell brass forever. The world is saying, "Fool me once, shame on you; fool me twice, you won't get a chance."

O what a tangled web we weave,
When first we practice to deceive.
—Sir Walter Scott

Let no man deceive himself.
—I Corinthians 3:18

Fences of Defense

To say that goodness, righteousness, civility and the Bible need no defense is captivating but wrong. The Apostle Paul said, "I am set for the defense of the gospel of Christ." He knew it should be defended. When there is no defense of right, wrong has a victory.

The best defenses are: (1) Strong conviction that you are right. The fixed mind fixes the course. (2) Faithful friend who will stand with you. A valiant associate fortifies. (3) To keep out of range until you are ready. If you can, you pick the time and the occasion. (4) To put on the whole armor of God. Be fully prepared. (5) And to mount a strong offense. This is the best defense.

Even the lion has to defend himself against flies.
—GERMAN PROVERB

Men, brethren, and fathers, hear ye my defense which I make now unto you.
—ACTS 22:1

When Rashness Rules

The mass of people lead lives of unstudied decisions, do only surface thinking. The results are failures, unfulfilled hopes, broken purses and broken hearts. Sufferings stalk the impulsive like a lion its prey.

When rashness rules the day, it is then that luck runs out. Or was it luck? Or was it the precipitation of hard times by one's own impetuous judgment? So it is highly imperative that we think. Weigh facts and arguments. Consider before we agree. Read before we sign. Visualize the end before we begin.

Later it will be most uncomfortable to break out with a rashness.

—ANONYMOUS

Yea, though a wise man think to know....
—ECCLESIASTES 8:17

Somebody Failed

We do not like to think about juvenile delinquency. We prefer to dwell on the positive and the pleasant. But delinquency is a reality, and a refusal to face it will not change it. Furthermore, reality suggests that we not put it all on youth. For there is adult remiss as well as juvenile failure, and the latter is due to the former: parents, teachers, preachers, civic leaders, government leaders, neighbors and businessmen. Someone failed!

Parents, we must train up our children in the way they should go, but we must go first. Then call back to them, for there are other calls they might heed.

All humans can go astray, but the young are more easily influenced.

—ANONYMOUS

Train up a child in the way he should go: and when he is old, he will not depart from it.

—PROVERBS 22:6

Learn to Wait

T here are maxims both for and against waiting, such as "Everything comes to those who can wait" and "He who waits for another man's platter has a cold meal." So evidently, the asset or liability of waiting depends on the circumstance. Just waiting for something to turn up is not beneficial. It is more productive to get a shovel and dig for it. Waiting is profitable only when it is wise waiting. In many areas success requires waiting. After the planting there must be a waiting period before the harvest. Impatience will not cause the seed to sprout and grow faster. It takes time to grow a tree. Learn to wait.

Learn to labor and to wait.
—HENRY WADSWORTH LONGFELLOW

...the husbandman waiteth for the precious fruit of the earth, and hath long patience for it.
—JAMES 5:7

Never Despair

In every life there must be some disappointments. They can be the stones, however, we climb to reach loftier heights. So let us accept them without forlornness. When despair looms because hopes are dashed, it is no time to give up and bow to broken dreams. Rather, it is a time to cry unto the Lord and renew ourselves.

The past may be lost, but the future still remains. The valley of despair is no place for you. Pack up your aspirations and ascend the mountain peak. It gives a longer view of a victorious life on the other side. That life can be yours! And mine!

At first I was almost about to despair, I thought I never could bear it—but I did bear it. The question remains: how?

—HEINRICH HEINE

Out of the depths have I cried unto thee, O Lord.

—PSALM 130:1

More Than a Living

May it never be said of any of us, "He made a living but never lived." Making a living is important but never as an end within itself—only as a means to living.

Life isn't a bed of roses, but it can be a rose garden. It will have some thorns that prick but also a thousand roses to adorn our paths and to provide a delightful aroma. Though life has its pricks, caution will lessen them. Also, gathering a few roses to hand to others will enliven us. And taking time to enjoy the rose-scented air will invigorate us. It is living.

Time hurries past thee like the breeze;
How swift its moments fly,
Make haste, O man! to live.
—HORATIUS BONAR

Forsake the foolish, and live....
—PROVERBS 9:6

A Pure Heart

The most important part of man for him to maintain is his heart. Spiritual heart. "For out of it are the issues of life." When kept, it provides immeasurable benefits in a regulated, orderly life. To keep it is to keep it in control.

In that domain called the human heart, there is the possibility for God or Satan to reign and give the orders. When both are heeded, a person sees with double eyes and zigzags in the path of life. The remedy is to unify life, and this is done by resolving and setting the heart. For "a man's heart deviseth his way."

My strength is as the strength of ten,
Because my heart is pure.
—ALFRED LORD TENNYSON

Keep thy heart with all diligence; for out of it are the issues of life.
—PROVERBS 4:23

Idols of Custom

Custom makes wrong acceptable and easy to
follow. Truly, holding to custom for custom's
sake makes idols of them. If customs are based on
Scripture, truth, morality, efficiency and right,
hold to them, hold to them tenaciously.

But if they grew out of error and wrong, started
by the blind and perpetuated by the blind, then
open your eyes and break those slavish holds.
There is no reason to continue doing anything
just because it has been done a long time. I need a
better reason. For unfounded custom is the plague
of religion, the slavery of the superstitious, and
the idol of the foolish.

Custom is almost second nature.

—PLUTARCH
(A.D. 46-120)

And it was a custom in Israel, that the daughters
of Israel went yearly to lament the daughter of
Jephthah the Gileadite four days in a year.

—JUDGES 11:39,40

Building Man Comes First

I t is important to build cities, schools, hospitals, factories, transportation systems, and other businesses; but our first duty is to build man. For no segment of our society can be stronger than the people who constitute it.

Construction requires a blueprint, labor and time. Also, in building a life, it takes a plan, thought, work and moreover a lifetime to make it the best. A solid foundation is needed. The taller the building, the deeper the foundation must go. If you would build your life high, first dig deep and lay a foundation. Additionally, the best of materials are essential: truthfulness, honesty, industry, goodness, love and faith. Then, piece by piece, put it together and watch it rise.

What a piece of work is man.
—WILLIAM SHAKESPEARE

Therefore whosoever heareth these sayings of mine, and doeth them, I will liken him unto a wise man, which built his house upon a rock....
—MATTHEW 7:24

A Prized Virtue

L oyalty is one of the most prized virtues. Further-more, a necessary requirement of success! Rela-tionships cannot last long on Judas loyalty. No person can win in the race of life on disloyal legs that zigzag here and there for momentary favor or temporary gain. We can't sell our friends short and come up long. We can't betray our religious principles and exemplify a character that demands respect.

Loyalty won't let us buy the truth and sell it to the highest bidder. It won't "hold with the hare and run with the hound." It will, however, let us switch sides when we see that we are wrong. For this is the highest loyalty: loyalty to right.

We mutually pledge to each other our lives, our fortunes, and our sacred honor.

—THOMAS JEFFERSON

As the cold of snow in the time of harvest, so is a faithful messenger to them that send him....

—PROVERBS 25:13

Disease of Hate

We should not hate other people. Never! What about their evils? Yes! We should hate falsehoods, deceptions, exploitations, betrayals and all other evils, but not the perpetrators. I know this is easier said than done. But be practical. Hating people is blinding, vengeful, conscience-searing and strife-making. It is as Harry Emerson Fosdick suggested, "Hating people is like burning down your house to get rid of a rat." It destroys the hater more than the hated. A disease that eats out the heart of its carrier!

And there is no medicine that will cure it but a good dose of the Word of God: "Love your enemies, bless them that curse you, do good to them that hate you."

I shall allow no man to belittle my soul by making me hate him.

—BOOKER T. WASHINGTON

Hatred stirreth up strifes: but love covereth all sins.

—PROVERBS 10:12

Wellspring of Life

When young people walk across the stage to get their diplomas, ordinarily their learning within a range does not vary too much. But bring your gauges fifty years later; oh! the differences are staggering.

Education is a continuous process, and the whole world is the classroom. This is why that fifty years later some are learned giants while others are only "sheepskin" holders.

We should learn from our experiences. A burned child is afraid of fire. If we don't learn from our mistakes, we have refused the world's best teacher. Also, we should learn from the mistakes of others, for we can't live long enough to make them all ourselves; furthermore, we are learning at their expense instead of ours.

Better learn late than never.

—GREEK PROVERB

Understanding is a wellspring of life unto him that hath it....

—PROVERBS 16:22

The Road to Happiness

All humans have happiness as their goal, but not all find it. The ways in which they seek it are as different as the people themselves. The road some take to find it actually takes them farther from it. The blissful state is never found in how much we have, but in how much we enjoy it; not in our role, but in how well we perform it; not in being served, but in serving; not in what others think of us, but in what we think of ourselves.

Happiness is simpler to find than most of us have ever realized. To find it, live a useful life, perform constructive jobs, blend your life with another or others, be unselfish, keep an approving conscience, make others happy, have something for which to hope, and trust in the Lord.

Man is the artificer of his own happiness.
—HENRY DAVID THOREAU

…whoso trusteth in the Lord, happy is he.
—PROVERBS 16:20

When Change Improves

T he world is undergoing changes. Some for the better. Some for the worse. So let us not think that all change is progress. Yet, all progress comes from change, but all change is not necessarily progress. For it to be progress, it depends on the change that is made: from wrong to right, from error to truth, from danger to safety, from slothfulness to diligence, and from ineptness to efficiency.

Practicality cries out that change should never be made for the sake of change. Make it only when improvement can be made; but when it can be made, turn loose of the old, the outdated and the inferior. For this is a necessary step to progress.

To change and change for the better are two different things.

—GERMAN PROVERB

For ye were sometimes darkness, but now are ye light in the Lord....

EPHESIANS 5:8

The Emptiness of Loneliness

Every person needs a little time each day to be alone. This time spent with an interesting person—YOU—does not have to be a lonely experience. It rather gives one undistracted time to think, meditate, ponder, plan and pray, all of which are very productive. Precious moments.

But loneliness is something else: emptiness. There is nothing to defy time and space. Nothing grips attention. No human ties (though you are in the midst of a million people) satisfy. This loneliness akin to death will occur unless we find satisfying company in things, causes or people. This being true, we need to cultivate an interest in the happenings of the day and put the doormat out to people.

How lonely we shall be!
What shall we do,
You without me,
I without you?

—HAROLD MONRO

Two are better than one....

—ECCLESIASTES 4:9

Made by Decisions

Decisions! Decisions! They weary us, for so much is dependent upon them. Today's decisions determine tomorrow's fate. We make the decisions, and then the decisions make us.

Where bad is the best, there is no choice. Look elsewhere. Study the matter thoroughly, look at it from every angle, turn it inside out, get the best available advice, sleep on it, and then decide. But don't wait too long. Don't let this life pass you by because you can't make up your mind.

And when once the decision is made, put it into effect. For decisions not executed are no better than non-decisions.

Take time to deliberate; but when the time for action arrives, stop thinking and go on.
—ANDREW JACKSON

So shall thy judgment be; thyself hast decided it.
—I KINGS 20:40

Liberty for All

L iberty—what a cherished word! Something for which many heroic figures have fought and sacrificed, bled and died. It hasn't come cheap. It shouldn't be given up lightly. Of course, it does have restrictions. For no person should have the liberty to do what he wishes if it hurts another. For instance, each person should have the freedom to wear artificial teeth; but if he should try to cram them down my throat, it becomes another matter.

Since no one lives unto himself, we must have laws for the good of all; but the more laws we pass, the more regimented we become and the less liberty we have. So moderation is needed.

Now for the fullest freedom, be not personally chained to that which would personally enslave you.

I pledge allegiance to the flag of the United States of America and to the republic for which it stands, one nation, under God, indivisible, with liberty and justice for all.

—THE PLEDGE OF ALLEGIANCE
FRANCIS BELLAMY

And Paul said, But I was free-born.

—ACTS 22:28

Rightly Rewarded

The law of compensation is divine. A long time ago Moses said, "Thou shalt not muzzle the ox when he treadeth out the corn" (Deuteronomy 25:4). If it is fair for the lowly beast to be compensated for his labors, then how much more right it is that the principle be applied to man.

It is an act of justice that work should be rewarded, that sowing should allow reaping, and that gathering should permit the partaking of it. This is equitable. If work is worthy of hire, then justice also says that more work is worthy of more hire. And if you work for money, then fair play declares that it is nothing but right that your money should be permitted to work for you. This is logical. This is ethical.

This is a world of compensation.
—ABRAHAM LINCOLN

...for the laborer is worthy of his hire.
—LUKE 10:7

More Than Conquerors

Though there are no waving flags, marching bands and eloquent speeches, the greatest hero is the victor over self. He struggled with his most hurtful enemy and won.

First he had to know self, which knowledge eludes many because they are blind and deaf to self. In the second place, conquest demands activity; passiveness conquers nothing—we have to do battle. And third, it takes persistence. If we occasionally lose a battle, don't lie in defeat. Rise to fight again and again and again.

Having conquered self, now we are ready to go up against the wrongs in a society that is in dire need of soldiers of right.

I came, I saw, I conquered.

—JULIUS CAESAR

Nay, in all these things we are more than conquerors through him that loved us.

—ROMANS 8:37

Righting Wrongs

Refusing to admit a wrong never rights it. Moreover, the unadmitted wrong is not likely to lie dormant. It is more apt to spread and multiply. Then what started out as a slight infraction grows into a monstrous corruption. To overcome the deficiency, there must be confession. It has been said that confession is good for the soul. Furthermore, it is good for human relations. It can unite the alienated.

To err is human, and to confess is closer to innocence. It is a salve for the conscience. It is a door to a bigger and fuller life. And well-bred people free of complexes have no problem acknowledging error.

A man should never be ashamed to own he has been wrong, which is but saying in other words, that he is wiser today than he was yesterday.
—ALEXANDER POPE

Confess your faults one to another, and pray one for another, that ye may be healed.
—JAMES 5:16

Motivated by Desire

E very person's desire motivates him. It gives zest and vigor to life. To cease desiring is to quit living and start dying. Reasonable desire can be reasonably attained provided the necessary thought and effort are put forth. For instance, if you would have fish, get a net and drop it in the water; if they are not there, pick another fishing hole.

We may never get all we want; the list may be too long for so few years. But actually, there is more peace in wanting what we get than in getting what we want. And there is more ecstasy in the chase than in the catch.

Thy wish was father to that thought.
—WILLIAM SHAKESPEARE

Thou hast given him his heart's desire, and hast not withholden the request of his lips.
—PSALM 21:2

Home Sweet Home

H ome is home, though it be ever so homely. And as it goes, so goes the world. If it's a proper, righteous one, it's more than a house. What gives it a fond memory is not boards and bricks, nor largeness and luxuries, but the tie of love. It ties our hearts together and makes all for one and one for all. The result is unity, happiness, security and hope, all found in the bond of home life.

Home shouldn't be a mere filling station. Not a debating society. Not a boxer's ring. Not hate's palace. It should be a place of love. And like the little birds grow up and leave the nest, the children grow up and depart, but their affections remain forever. For it is home.

Home is where there's one to love us.
—CHARLES SWAIN

Return to thine own house, and show how great things God hath done unto thee.
-—LUKE 8:39

From the Ears Up

The most important part of man is from his ears up. That is the part that understands, thinks, reasons, loves, plans, pursues, makes the real money (from the ears down makes only a bare living), spends the money, goes to church and prepares to meet God.

Therefore, a good head is better than a thousand hands. Now for a superior head—greater than mere intellect—fill it full of God's Word and wisdom, and as it comes out you shall be directed in green pastures with still waters.

Some men have heads, but they are not particularly furnished.

—WOODROW WILSON

The wise man's eyes are in his head....

—ECCLESIASTES 2:14

Should We Prosper?

Our very nature—creatures in the image of God, a little lower than the angels—befits a delightful birth and a life of plenty. It is our birthright. To think otherwise contradicts the design of all the earth. Unequivocally, man the best of God's creation should not be expected to live on the worst.

While material prosperity meets one of our needs, it is certainly not the whole of life. "Man shall not live by bread alone." However, the passage does suggest that man does live by bread, but not by bread alone; that's the point. God wants us to prosper. Furthermore, He has laid out a blueprint in the Bible that tells us what to do, how and why. This is motivating.

Poverty is very good in poems but very bad in the house, very good in maxims and sermons but very bad in practical life.

—Henry Ward Beecher

...I wish above all things that thou mayest prosper and be in health, even as thy soul prospereth.

—III John 2

The Contentment That Blesses

When we don't have what we like, it is advantageous to like what we have—until we can do better. And as Shakespeare said, such "content is our best having." Contentment is not a state of no desire, however, but one that is not disquieted and disturbed in the pursuit of that desire. For instance, a farmer's desire causes him to plant, but content lets him live in peace during the planting, growing and harvesting seasons.

Free of frustration, contentment preserves our energy for the necessary talks rather than drain it off unnecessarily to no accomplishment. As William George Jordan has said, "There are times when a man should be content with what he has, but never with what he is."

Content makes poor men rich; discontent makes rich men poor.

—BENJAMIN FRANKLIN

But godliness with contentment is great gain.

—I TIMOTHY 6:6

Making Life Worth Living

L ife is largely what we make it—with God's help. Life consists of days, but real life consists of more—that which makes the days worthwhile. Indeed, it includes more than breaths, figures on a dial and numbers on a calendar.

Life is a gift—be grateful. Meant to be lived a day at a time—never lose a day. Meant to be simple—don't complicate it. Meant to be lovely— avoid the ugly. Meant to be happy—don't bring miseries upon it. Meant to be a responsibility— face it. Meant to be a success—be a good student. Meant to be continued—otherwise nothing would be permanently accomplished and the work of the Creator would end in failure.

What life in the long run does to us depends on what life finds in us.
—HARRY EMERSON FOSDICK

...a man's life consisteth not in the abundance of the things which he possesseth.
—LUKE 12:15

Living Epitaphs

Epitaphs are known to pervert facts and to stretch truth. Sympathy seeks to say good things about a person, and especially when he's down. This comes easily, for we are inclined to bury the person's faults with him. Of course, giving just a little sugar now when one is living is better than a lot of taffy when he is dead.

The personal application of all this is to so live that the epitaph writer won't be tempted to be a prevaricator. Actually, the living people we have helped are the best epitaphs; they say more about us than flowery words engraved on cold headstones.

Here lies one who walked not perfectly but humbly with his God, did some things right, some things wrong, but always meant well—an epitaph good enough for a king.

—ANONYMOUS

Blessed are the dead which die in the Lord…they may rest from their labors; and their works do follow them.

—REVELATION 14:13

Coals of Fire

This is an unpleasant topic, but it is practical, Biblical and needs attention. For we all have enemies. So, how do we handle the problem?

First, pray for them. Jesus did.

Second, return good for evil. This heaps coals of fire on their head, which is better than meeting enmity with enmity. Furthermore, hateful reaction to an enemy makes one his own worst enemy. Don't let vengeful rancor destroy you.

Third, possessed with goodwill, we should go forward with the faith that God is bigger than our enemies and can bless us even in their presence, as David stated, "Thou preparest a table before me in the presence of mine enemies."

I destroy my enemy when I make him my friend.

—ABRAHAM LINCOLN

Therefore if thine enemy hunger, feed him; if he thirst, give him drink....

—ROMANS 12:20

Being Thankful

Since we are not God and cannot do everything for ourselves, then we ought to be thankful for what God and others do for us. That's fair. That's big. That's noble. That's recognition. That's so different from the spirit that receives and receives and never says thanks, at least not aloud.

Thankfulness makes personality shine and keeps morale from lagging. It's easier to bear what we don't have if we're grateful for what we do have. It keeps us from sinking into despair and pessimism, encourages us to renew our efforts, and heartens us to continue in the pursuit of our dreams. It even shows in the face, giving it a warm glow and a cheerful smile.

An easy thing, O Power Divine,
To thank Thee for these gifts of Thine.
—THOMAS WENTWORTH HIGGINSON

...abounding therein with thanksgiving.
—COLOSSIANS 2:7

Hold On

H old on with bulldog grit. Every trying task can be accomplished only by hanging in there. Every bitter fate is to be overcome—if overcomeable— by endurance; and if it cannot be surmounted, then it is to be handled by resignation, patience and perseverance. In either case, to do this, deep faith and commitment are essential. Shallow ponds dry up fast, and trees with shallow roots go down first in the storm.

The twin bears of victory are bear and forbear. What is bitter to endure is sweet to conquer. Then the triumph is so pleasant because the struggle was so trying.

Nothing befalls any man which he is not fitted to endure.

—GREEK PROVERB

...he that endureth to the end shall be saved.

—MATTHEW 10:22

Known by Our Company

Here is one of the most thoughtful questions you will ever answer: Are your friends and companions pulling you up or pulling you down? A degenerate companionship is like a dirty dog who dirties those he rubs against. Evil association can steal more than time; it can be the thief of character. But wholesome association makes bad people good and good people better.

As a general rule, we know a person by the company he keeps, for like attracts like. Wolves go in packs, cattle graze in herds, and people run with those of similar views and goals. This being true, tell me the company you keep, and I'll tell you the person you are.

He that lies down with dogs will rise up with fleas.

—LATIN PROVERB

He that walketh with wise men shall be wise: but a companion of fools shall be destroyed.

—PROVERBS 13:20

Thanksgiving

We should all be rich in thanks. This virtue has set our pioneer fathers apart and given them a praiseworthy place in history—the founders of Thanksgiving Day.

May we their grateful offspring ever be proud of this heritage and continue in the same spirit that prompted it.

WHEREAS it is the duty of all nations to acknowledge the providence of Almighty God, to obey His will, to be grateful for His benefit, and humbly implore His protection, aid and favors...

Now, THEREFORE, I do recommend and assign Thursday, the 26th Day of November next, to be devoted by the people of these states to the service of that great and glorious Being, who is the Beneficent Author of all the good that was, that is, or that will be; that we may then all unite in rendering unto Him our sincere and humble thanks for His kind care and protection of the people of this country, and for all the great and various favors which He has been pleased to confer upon us.

—First Thanksgiving Proclamation
By George Washington, 1789

Enter into his gates with thanksgiving, and into his courts with praise.

—Psalm 100:4

Is It Really Defeat?

Defeat and feat are sometimes close together, and one can change into the other. So defeat is only what a person makes it.

Defeat can be the crushing of an ambition, the end of a struggle, the acceptance of a minor role, and even the transformation of one into a walking corpse.

On the other hand, it can be a look to another day, a renewal of will, a remaking of plans, and a fresh stimulus to greater efforts.

If the latter is true, then defeat is not defeat. Just cessation. The war goes on, and the outcome is not determined by one battle. Fight on! Fight on!

But in ourselves are triumph and defeat.
— HENRY WADSWORTH LONGFELLOW

We are troubled on every side, yet not distressed; we are perplexed, but not in despair; persecuted, but not forsaken; cast down, but not destroyed.
— II CORINTHIANS 4:8,9

Sharper Than a Serpent's Tooth

One blemish on our society is ingratitude. Favors are accepted but not appreciated. Eaten bread goes unthanked. Helpfulness is forgotten. This despicable trait is the outgrowth of two other dreadful faults: selfishness and pride. The ingrate finds it hard to say "thank you": First, he thinks he deserves the benefit and should get more. Second, he has too much pride to acknowledge his being in debt to anyone.

Indeed, it is hard to bear the callous ingratitude of people we have helped, but really that's their problem. Our problem is to rise above their unthankfulness, keep our own charitable disposition and continue in good works.

How sharper than a serpent's tooth it is,
To have a thankless child.
—WILLIAM SHAKESPEARE

For men shall be lovers of their own selves...proud...unthankful....
—II TIMOTHY 3:2

Getting Even

The best way to get even is to lift the fallen. And the best way to thaw another is to be warm. It is the madness of folly for unbending rigor to demand "an eye for an eye, and a tooth for a tooth." For with the same measure we mete, it shall be measured to us again.

The sooner we recognize we need leniency, the sooner we will show it to others. Being brothers in fallibility, we should be too big for retaliation. Returning good for evil has double benefits: blesses the people who do and the people who receive. It testifies to a kind spirit.

For mere vengeance I would do nothing. This nation is too great to look for mere revenge. But for the security of the future I would do everything.

—JAMES A. GARFIELD

Not rendering evil for evil, or railing for railing: but contrariwise blessing....

—I PETER 3:9

The Laurels of Fame

There is no downhill road to the glories of fame; it's all climb. And he who climbs its heights must climb above those who are content to remain at the lower levels. The climb takes inspiration and perspiration, a wonderful combination of thinking it out and sweating it out.

Since the laurels of fame are bestowed by others, then it can be elusive and fleeting. A fickle mob may raise us up today, but at the slightest whim cast us down tomorrow. Flip-floppers are expressive of cheers at sunrise but jeers at sundown. Either cheers or jeers gives them an outlet to their emotions. Fame, how vain! Just a hollow echo! It is consoling, therefore, that fame is not a requirement of heaven. Whether the world recognizes us or not, God sees. And that's what really counts.

Fame is a fickle food
Upon a shifting plate.

—EMILY DICKINSON

So the Lord was with Joshua; and his fame was noised throughout all the country.

—JOSHUA 6:27

Count the Cost

What costs little is usually prized little. What we pay for in blood, sweat and tears is esteemed highly. However, what costs the most is not always the most valuable, and the least expensive is not always the cheapest.

This is where wisdom is needed for one to be the most efficient in making the exchange. We obtain one thing at the cost of giving up something else. Family, freedom, education, health, wealth, spirituality, good citizenship, success, and every other blessed estate has a price tag. But to buy the opposites will actually cost much more and be worth much less.

The altar of accomplishment has always been stacked with sacrifices.

—ANONYMOUS

Nay; but I will surely buy it of thee at a price....
—II SAMUEL 24:24

Truly Educated

F ew things are worth as much as a correctly instructed mind. This being true, superior and lofty education should have priority in the land. Ignorance holds people in bondage, and the way to be free is to know.

The school of fastest learning is the School of Hard Knocks. The tuition is extremely high, but the students learn fast.

The fullest and most rounded education for children is the fourfold kind Jesus received, which was intellectual, physical, religious and social. This covers the whole field.

A child educated only at school is an uneducated child.

—GEORGE SANTAYANA

And Jesus increased in wisdom and stature, and in favor with God and man.

—LUKE 2:52

Gracious Hospitality

T he disposition to kindly and generously entertain guests and strangers is a noble attribute. A rewarding one. Even if there should be no reciprocation, it still pays because it is so personally exhilarating. Hospitality is more than the sharing of home, preparation, food and time; basically, it is the sharing of self, a mark of love, a love that bids welcome.

Understandably, the world loves a host or hostess. In an increasingly self-centered society, hospitality is not as much in vogue as it once was. We need to get back to it.

He was a wealthy man, and kindly to his fellow men, for dwelling in a house by the side of the road, he used to entertain all comers.

—HOMER
(700 B.C.)

Use hospitality one to another without grudging.
—I PETER 4:9

Give Your Ears a Chance

"I like him because he listens well," stated one man in explaining his appreciation of another. Listening makes friends. Give them your ears and they will seek your presence and give you their hearts. But slow, dull ears and a fast, over-greased tongue will drive away crowds and leave a person lonely. Truly, an imbalance of nature—too much tongue and not enough ears. A serious handicap!

Listen to get smarter, to get direction, to get another view, to save embarrassment, to stay out of trouble, and to be appreciated. Of course, logic says that for somebody to listen, somebody else has to talk. But keep it in balance.

A good listener is not only popular everywhere, but after a while he gets to know something.
—WILSON MIZNER

...let every man be swift to hear, slow to speak....
—JAMES 1:19

Faith Is

F aith is to life what gasoline is to a motor: the energizing power that makes it go. Thus the greatest accomplishments are the accomplishments of faith. It is what we believe we can do—with God's help—that sows the seed, builds the house, opens the business, takes up the cause, finishes the race, climbs the ladder, or heads to the moon.

I like its "I can" atmosphere. I also like its results. So long as we have faith, we shall be able to meet today's certainties and tomorrow's unknowns. Knowing that the victorious life is one of faith, we beseech our Maker, "Help thou mine unbelief."

Faith is to believe what we do not see, and the reward of this faith is to see what we believe.

—St. Augustine

...and this is the victory that overcometh the world, even our faith.

—I John 5:4

The Mirror of the Heart

A good-looking face is only a half fortune. And the greater half is the heart; however, the heart does express itself in the face. Like a mirror, the face reflects the heart, and the eyes without speaking say much.

Hence, it is not what is on the face but what is in the face that reaches to the heart that makes the greatest difference. There we can have the marks of inner conditions which glow with an unexcelled beauty. If we weren't born beautiful, we can blame our ancestors; but if we are still unattractive at fifty, it is our fault.

It has been said of an attractive woman, "There is a garden in her face where roses and white lilies grow."

Every right action and true thought sets the seal of its beauty on the person and the face.
—JOHN RUSKIN

A man's wisdom maketh his face to shine.
—ECCLESIASTES 8:1

Open My Eyes

The forerunners and accomplishers have eyes that see. For what we see has a very pronounced bearing on life. Open eyes can keep us off Stupidity Street.

The lofty life is realized by first seeing with lofty eyes. Downcast eyes miss opportunities. "Lift up your eyes and look on the fields."

The very reason some never see God is that "their eyes they have closed." Consequently they fail to see the greatest source of help. "I will lift up mine eyes unto the hills, from whence cometh my help." Thus it is appropriate to pray, "God, let me see."

Are we disposed to be the number of those who, having eyes, see not?

—PATRICK HENRY

Open thou mine eyes, that I may behold wondrous things out of thy law.

—PSALM 119:18

Strengthened by Convictions

T he person who has no convictions has nothing, nothing to sustain him, nothing to guide him, nothing to stabilize him. He is only putty in the hands of people and circumstances. He will hunt with anybody's dog. Go with the wind. He will subordinate moral and religious principles for the sake of facilitating a purpose. He may go to church, but only to rob the altar. He should not be trusted for he has nothing to trust.

Every person owes it to himself to be something, to believe something, and to stand for something. It takes courage, but this is one of the high privileges of the soul. Be not afraid of nonconformity; it can be your distinction of valor.

The only faith that wears well and holds its color in all weathers is that which is woven of conviction.

—JAMES RUSSELL LOWELL

And all the king's servants, that were in the king's gate, bowed, and reverenced Haman: for the king had so commanded concerning him. But Mordecai bowed not, nor did him reverence.

—ESTHER 3:2

Futility of Excuses

Be straightforward. Don't make an excuse. A reason? Yes, sometimes. An excuse? No! Never! Some excuses are too ridiculous and silly for intelligent people to make. And for intelligent people to accept. Pretexts can always be found if one wishes to hide behind them. But the public can see through them. Then why do people make them? Because it seems the easy way out. Because reasonableness gets lost in self-centeredness.

And the modern excuses are no improvement over the old ones, just about the same, which have already been heard again and again by the old-timers. What rubbish! How futile!

Actually, the excuser becomes his own accuser.

And oftentimes excusing of a fault
Doth make the fault the worse by the excuse.
—WILLIAM SHAKESPEARE

And they all with one consent began to make excuse.

—LUKE 14:18

An Ounce of Practice

T he greatest preacher is example. An ounce of practice is worth a pound of oratory. Living a sermon is a seminary within itself.

One example is worth a hundred sermons. My eyes that see the sermon in practice learn faster than my ears that hear it in precept. We may question the words but not the deeds. The most effective way to bring up children in the upright way is to walk ahead of them. Kids follow.

Whether we like it or not, we are the "Bible" some people read. What do they see? Are they attracted or repulsed?

I'd rather see a sermon than hear one any day,
I'd rather one should walk with me than merely
tell the way.

—EDGAR A. GUEST

...be thou an example of the believers, in word, in conversation, in charity, in spirit, in faith, in purity.

—I TIMOTHY 4:12

Tall Tales

If it weren't for exaggeration, most fish stories would hardly be worth telling. But laying all jokes aside, overstatement does cause a person to lose credibility. And it does put one over into the class of, yes, prevaricators. Now, we can tone that down a little by saying truth-stretchers or falsehood-tellers.

Whatever we call it, no person can build himself up by building up the story he tells. So don't let a tall story shorten you. Good things don't have to be exaggerated, and the bad things are bad enough without it.

There are people so addicted to exaggeration that they can't tell the truth without lying.

—JOSH BILLINGS

...whose mouth speaketh vanity, and their right hand is a right hand of falsehood.

—PSALM 144:8

What Makes the Haves

Wise and efficient saving makes the haves. Without it, no earnings are enough. Frugality is a great revenue for it doesn't take so much money when waste is eliminated and efficiency is exercised in the spending of it. Samuel Johnson correctly stated, "Without economy none can be rich, and with it few can be poor."

Efforts to economize indicate other excellencies: appreciation of God's gifts, sense of values, forethought, efficiency, self-denial, prudence, vision and a well-regulated mind. Truly, economy says much and is worthy of much credit. When Jesus commanded that the fragments be gathered up, He made it compulsory.

Economy is too late at the bottom of the purse.
—LATIN PROVERB

When they were filled, he said unto his disciples, Gather up the fragments that remain, that nothing be lost.
—JOHN 6:12

Accepting Duty

Duty is a requirement of progress—and even existence. The big problem is personal duty, bigger than public duty. And there is no way to handle duties but to discharge them. Dodged duties are like dodged debts, not paid, only deferred, and thereby leave the irresponsible severely harmed.

It is easy for minor matters to divert us from our major obligations. Never allow it. Priority forbids it. Life is duty, and just to wake up finds it all around us. Wake up! See it! Accept it! And in so doing, we shall sip from our own cup of blessing.

You can never do more than your duty; you should never wish to do less.

—ROBERT E. LEE

Let us hear the conclusion of the whole matter: Fear God, and keep his commandments: for this is the whole duty of man.

—ECCLESIASTES 12:13

A Time to Be Earnest

One can have a serious mind and a sober outlook on life without mummifying personality. Solomon stated that there is "a time to weep, and a time to laugh," a time for somber considerations and a time for lighter moments. Hence, earnestness and wit can and should be intermingled.

Since life is earnest, then no person devoid of it ever becomes great. He may be clever and entertaining, but he lacks depth. Earnestness is born of convictions. It has a touch that moves people. The world is more anxious to feel us than to hear us.

Life is real! Life is earnest!
  And the grave is not its goal;
Dust thou art, to dust returnest,
  Was not spoken of the soul.
                    —HENRY WADSWORTH LONGFELLOW

Therefore we ought to give the more earnest heed to the things which we have heard, lest at any time we should let them slip.
                              —HEBREWS 2:1

By Chance or Choice

Uncontrollable circumstances have a bearing; but largely speaking, each is the master of his own destiny. Each is his own star of fate. It's not a matter of chance, but a matter of choice. Choices become actions, and actions take us along the road of destiny.

The helpless passivist says, "What will be will be." But the optimistic activist says, "What I choose and do I become." Julius Caesar said, "The die is cast." If so, we cast it; and if we don't like the casting, we can start over and re-cast it. God will do His part. Now it is up to each of us.

In the field of destiny, we reap as we have sown.
—JOHN GREENLEAF WHITTIER

...whatsoever a man soweth, that shall he also reap.
—GALATIANS 6:7

Just Do It

S tatues are built to doers, not just mere dreamers or vain talkers. They are our heroes and our heroines. They are our examples. The only thing that really counts is what we do. The world wants a job done, not just talked about. And so does God!

Doers walk through the door of opportunity. They have more than an existence—a full life, one that pulsates with interest, challenge and satisfaction. It is gratifying to perform well.

Cultivate the spirit of doing by applying Solomon's advice: "Whatsoever thy hand findeth to do, do it with thy might." Give the best you have, and the best will come back to you.

The more we do, the more we can do; the more busy we are, the more leisure we have.
—WILLIAM HAZLITT

But be ye doers of the word, and not hearers only, deceiving your own selves.
—JAMES 1:22

A Matter of Heart

A college professor stated in class, "I'm sure that one sin is just as bad as another in the sight of God; but if one sin could be worse than another, I'm sure it would be the sin of disposition."

Unforgiveness. Vengeance. Hate. Spite. Envy. Selfishness. Pride. Meddlesomeness. Covetousness. All of these ugly qualities are sins of disposition and need to be replaced with love, goodwill, humility, tolerance, forgiveness, thoughtfulness, big-heartedness, kindness and a sunny spirit. And this can be done by keeping the heart, for out of it come the qualities that make temperament.

Beauty, Madame, pleases the eyes only;
sweetness of disposition charms the soul.

—VOLTAIRE

...what lack I yet?

—MATTHEW 19:20

Developing Character

Character is more supportive than intellect. For it gives brains something to work with. Without character, intellect is robbed of the supports that are needed. Our brains are born with us, though uneducated, but character is something we develop. It is put together by what we believe. As we believe in and follow the noblest principles of responsibility, dependability, integrity, consideration of others, morality and religion, they become ourselves.

To get a view of a person's real character, see him when he thinks no one is watching. Also, catch him off guard; then his real self comes out. Reputation is what people think of us. Character is what we are.

The measure of a man's real character is what he would do if he knew he never would be found out.

—Thomas Babington Macaulay

Jesus saw Nathanael coming to him, and saith of him, Behold an Israelite indeed, in whom is no guile!

—John 1:47

Little Things

It may be we don't put enough importance on little things. Perhaps it is more realistic to say, "Since little things have such far-reaching consequences, then there are no little things." Little raindrops—large ocean. Little acorn—mighty oak. Little leak—broken dam. Little kindness—great help. Little sin—long step. Little improvement— big trend.

Small matters show the real person, while big concerns may show only a feigned character. It appears that some are unaware that God notices the minutest things of life, for "a cup of cold water"—a little thing—given "in the name of a disciple" is worthy of His reward.

How far that little candle throws his beams!
So shines a good deed in a naughty world.
—WILLIAM SHAKESPEARE

Behold, how great a matter a little fire kindleth!
—JAMES 3:5

Dignity of Discretion

Sometimes courage says, Fight, when discretion says, Don't. This means that discretion can be the better part of valor. Temper says, Explode, but discretion says, Simmer. Loose thinking says, Tell all, but discretion says, Keep your troubles from going public. The flesh says, Gratify yourself, but discretion listens to another voice.

Evil invites, but discretion flees from the very appearance of it. Foolishness thinks only of the present, but discretion thinks of tomorrow. Discretion is a wise man's word, but indiscretion belongs to fools.

Philosophy is nothing but discretion.
— JOHN SELDEN

As a jewel of gold in a swine's snout, so is a fair woman which is without discretion.
— PROVERBS 11:22

Wings of Failure

L et us turn our failures into wings, not leaden shoes. The greatest failure is the failure to try. The second is to fail and not try again. Actually, no one has failed until he has ceased to try again. No person has suffered failure who learns from his nonsuccesses, rises from them, and tries again with renewed determination and dogged effort. Failure is not failure when it teaches a better way and prods another try at it. Getting back up just one more time than you get knocked down makes you a winner.

A failure is a man who has blundered but is not able to cash in the experience.

—ELBERT HUBBARD

...let the people renew their strength....

—ISAIAH 41:1

Expert Assistance

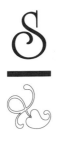

Sometimes we have jokingly said: An expert is a little spurt under pressure, or a little spurt from out of town, or a little spurt smart enough to tell you how to run your business but not smart enough to run his own.

Really, there is more to it, and an expert can be very efficient and credible. While a well-informed person knows a little about many things, an expert knows much about one thing. That is the difference. And when you get into an unfamiliar field, it is good to get the assistance of a specialist. That's why when a tooth aches we go to a dentist, not a mechanic. But when we need Biblical information and counseling that might not be the dentist's expertise, try the preacher or another person trained in this field.

Believe one who has proved it. Believe an expert.
—VIRGIL
(70-19 B.C.)

...I know thee to be expert in all customs and questions which are among the Jews....
—ACTS 26:3

Majority Rules

The right or wrong of a thing cannot be determined by consensus of opinion. If a thing is wrong, it is still wrong though the whole world accepts it.

Naturally we must allow the majority to have their way, but we must not allow them to take over our conscience. That is ours and ours to keep. Look what would have happened if we had been living in Noah's day and had gone with the majority. The masses have often demonstrated little virtue; and the virtue, if found at all, had to be found in smaller groups with wiser discernment. It is sad, but sometimes the majority is only a partisan group formed by self-serving men with little morals, big ambitions and loud voices.

A man with God is always in the majority.
—JOHN KNOX

Thou shalt not follow a multitude to do evil....
—EXODUS 23:2

The Basis of Civilization

C ivilization—this is humanity in a state of civility, social culture and well-being. And to get to this desired and exalted state, there must be a recognition of the sovereignty of God and a subjection to His laws. The long history of man testifies to this truth. If we have nothing to control us but our desire for a mess of flesh, we live on the cannibal's level.

Through the ages the nations that have forgotten God have suffered ruination and downfall. A departure from His righteous principles causes any nation, no matter how strong, to die from within. Righteousness exalts a nation. Thus godliness is the surest form of patriotism.

There is no solid basis for civilization but in the Word of God.

—DANIEL WEBSTER

The wicked shall be turned into hell, and all the nations that forget God.

—PSALM 9:17

Spirit of Christmas

T hough we don't know the exact day Christ was born, the world celebrates it today. His birth was humble, and His death was criminal albeit He did no crime.

When He was born, wise men from the East saw His star over Bethlehem and went to worship Him, taking gifts. May we also be wise enough to hitch our wagon to a star—the Star of Bethlehem.

Gifts are meaningful. Wise men thought so. Indeed, it is an outpouring of wisdom and appreciation that we give gifts. Most of them have to be bought, which creates traffic in the marketplace at Christmastime. But let's forget the commercialism and appreciate the spirit that prompted the purchase. It is a beautiful time of the year, with more kindness, more getting together, more giving, and more forgiving. Wouldn't it be wonderful if that spirit could last?

Just a little baby,
  Jesus was His name,
Bringing joy and gladness
  when from heaven He came.

—AUTHOR UNKNOWN

...they presented unto him gifts; gold, and frankincense, and myrrh.

—MATTHEW 2:11

Known by Deeds

There is a lot of difference between saying and doing. Talk comes cheap; it's the performance that has a price. Jesus' statement, "They say, and do not," has always characterized a certain element in our population.

Most assuredly the smallest deed is better than the biggest talk. And the most convincing answer is doing. The world may wonder about our speech but not about our deeds. Just as a tree is known by its fruit, a person is known by his deeds. Deed is the best creed; it shows the faith.

Give me the ready hand rather than the ready tongue.

—GIUSEPPE GARIBALDI

For every tree is known by his own fruit.

—LUKE 6:44

A Glorious Church

Some people who get nearer to church get farther from God, and some "who build God a church laugh his word to scorn"; but don't you think these are the exceptions? And don't you think fairness demands that we should no more condemn a whole church for a few of its members than we should judge a whole barrel of apples for a few rotten ones?

The church is made up of humans, and therefore it has some sin; but this is also a challenge—a challenge for each of us to become better than the unexemplary member and to shine a little brighter to make up for his gone-out candle.

Though the church has imperfections, think how much worse the world would be without it.

No sooner is a temple built to God but the Devil builds a chapel hard by.

—GEORGE HERBERT

...that he might present it to himself a glorious church, not having spot or wrinkle, or any such thing; but that it should be holy and without blemish.

—EPHESIANS 5:27

What About Discipline?

No person becomes great by turning himself loose and doing as he pleases. The horse needs a bridle and a spur. So does man. A soldier isn't developed by an exercise in smelling roses. Drills that are harder and rougher make him a tougher man.

It was strict discipline that made our forefathers a hardy people; it is an undisciplined, powder-puff philosophy that has weakened some of their descendants. The best discipline is self-discipline. For where self-control is lacking, self-created failure is sure. We must learn the what, the when, the where and the how much of life, to bridle ourselves, to spur our loins, to know when to give ourselves the reins and when to hold back.

It is never wise to slip the bonds of discipline.
—LEW WALLACE

...thou didst...chasten thyself before thy God....
—DANIEL 10:12

A Heart to Win

Success and failure in the everyday affairs of life are often not far apart, and determination can change the outcome. There is so much difference between half a heart and a whole heart that it controls man's destiny. A person without determination is self-defeated. He does not have the heart to win.

Determination is a kind of genius all its own—may be weak in education but strong in intensity. It will carry a person to heights that education alone will never take him. It knows no defeat. It tries again and again. And when one is at the end of his rope, determination ties a knot at the end and hangs on. It is the spirit of a conqueror.

The truest wisdom, in general, is a resolute determination.

—NAPOLEON

Then answered I them, and said unto them, The God of heaven, he will prosper us; therefore we his servants will arise and build.

—NEHEMIAH 2:20

Making Impossibility Possible

I mpossible in nearly every case can be spelled I'm-Possible. Napoleon said, "Impossible—that is not French." Impossible is an often-spoken word of the defeatists. It describes a condition of the heart: lost heart.

Of course, there are some things impossible for man, but most things considered impossible are not. They are only challenges. And what seems impossible gives way as knowledge is gained and effort is multiplied. Doing what others find difficult is talent; doing what others find impossible is genius. In rising each morning, let this thought motivate: "It's God's world, and I'm rising to a world of possibilities."

Do not think that what is hard for thee to master is impossible for man.

—Chang Heng
(A.D. 78-139)

...help thou mine unbelief.

—MARK 9:24

As the Year Ends

Swift time drives us to turn the calendar. Another year has slipped by. And to what avail? Where does it leave us? What about our victories? Our defeats? Truly, years teach more than books. Each passing year takes something from us but gives something in return. Takes a little muscle and stamina but adds knowledge, growth, depth and insight. If the spiritual is more important than the physical, then the swap has been advantageous.

No, the years don't have to pass like a dream. They can leave us with reality—a real past that is glorious upon which we can build a real future that is even more glorious. That makes every year a better year.

The years teach much which the days never know.

—RALPH WALDO EMERSON

I said, Days should speak, and multitude of years should teach wisdom.

—JOB 32:7